A SEVERED HEAD

A Severed Head

A play in three Acts
by

IRIS MURDOCH
and
J. B. PRIESTLEY

1964
Chatto & Windus
London

PUBLISHED BY
CHATTO AND WINDUS LTD
42 WILLIAM IV STREET
LONDON WC2

★

CLARKE, IRWIN AND CO LTD
TORONTO

PRINTED IN GREAT BRITAIN BY
T. H. BRICKELL AND SON LTD
THE BLACKMORE PRESS, GILLINGHAM, DORSET

Characters

in order of their appearance

MARTIN LYNCH-GIBBON, a wine merchant

GEORGIE HANDS, a young lecturer at London University, his mistress

ANTONIA, Martin's wife

PALMER ANDERSON, a psychoanalyst

ROSEMARY, Martin's sister

ALEXANDER, Martin's brother, a sculptor

HONOR KLEIN, Palmer's half-sister, an anthropologist

This reading edition of *A Severed Head* is an expanded version of the text used at the Criterion Theatre, and is not an acting version.

The first performance in Great Britain of *A Severed Head* was given at the Theatre Royal, Bristol on Tuesday, 7th May, 1963 by The Bristol Old Vic Company. It was directed by Val May, and designed by Graham Barlow. The cast was as follows:

MARTIN LYNCH-GIBBON	Robert Hardy
GEORGIE HANDS	Monica Evans
ANTONIA	Heather Chasen
PALMER ANDERSON	Paul Eddington
ROSEMARY	Barbara Leigh-Hunt
ALEXANDER	Christopher Benjamin
HONOR KLEIN	Sheila Burrell

The action takes place in London and passes between Georgie Hands' lodgings near Covent Garden, the sitting room of the Lynch-Gibbons' house in Hereford Square and the study and bedroom of Palmer Anderson's house in Chester Square. The time is the present.

ACT I

SCENE I

A foggy afternoon in December at GEORGIE HANDS' *lodgings. An untidy bookish bed-sittingroom full of bric-a-brac with a few posters pinned to the wall, and now decorated with desultory sprigs of holly. A litter of bottles, glasses, ash-trays. Fancy wrapping paper lies about from a recent exchange of presents. A gas-fire and three red candles on the mantelpiece afford the only light. In the background is a tousled single bed.*

GEORGIE *is an attractive clever-looking girl of twenty-six with a dry ironical manner. She has a broad face, strong rather than delicate, a pale complexion, an upturned nose, and plenty of long straight dark hair. She has had all her clothes off and has not yet put more than half of them on again.*

MARTIN *is a cheerful humorous man of forty-one, with a long old-fashioned English face and floppy light brown hair. He has not yet put on his coat, tie and shoes.*

The two lie half-embraced in front of the fire.

GEORGIE: I've been thinking.

MARTIN: About what?

GEORGIE: Are you *sure* she doesn't know?

MARTIN: Antonia? You mean about us? Certain.

GEORGIE [*slowly*]: Good. . . . I suppose . . . [*Pause.*] When must you go, darling?

MARTIN: Five at the latest, angel.

GEORGIE [*looking at him*]: Don't let me catch you being mean with time.

MARTIN: All right – all right – all right. [*He ruffles her hair.*] Antonia's psychoanalytic session ends at five. I ought to get back pretty soon after that. She always wants to discuss it in tremendous detail. [*He plays*

9

with her hair, spreading it carefully over her shoulders.]

GEORGIE [*rather drily*]: How *is* Antonia's psychoanalysis?

MARTIN: Going fizzingly. She enjoys it quite disgrace-
fully. I used to think an analysis was a sort of penitential business, but Antonia just goes on getting more
and more pleased with herself. Of course it's all for
fun really, she doesn't *need* it. But she's got a tremendous transference. Adores her analyst.

GEORGIE: Mmmm. Palmer Anderson. Yes, I can imagine being addicted to him.

MARTIN: You never told me you knew him.

GEORGIE: I don't. But I saw him once at a party in
Cambridge. His sister – or half-sister or step-sister,
whatever she is to him – gave the party, and she was
my supervisor that year. He looked amusing – attractive. And I imagine he's good at his trade.

MARTIN: I don't know about that. I must say I dislike
what you call his trade. But he's certainly good at
something. Perhaps he's just good.

GEORGIE: Do you mean clever or virtuous?

MARTIN: Both. Neither. Something else. He's not just
sweet and polite and gentle in that special way some
Americans have – but I feel he has real power in him.
He's certainly made a difference to me.

GEORGIE: In what way?

MARTIN: I think – he's made me worry less about the
rules.

GEORGIE [*laughs*]: The rules? Dear darling, surely you
became indifferent to the rules ages ago?

MARTIN: Good God – no! I'm not indifferent to them
now. I'm not a little savage like you, a little Cambridge child of nature. No, it's not quite that. But
Palmer's somehow good at – setting people free.

GEORGIE: If you think *I* don't worry about those rules –

ah, never mind. As for setting people free, I must say I don't trust these professional liberators. Anyone who's good at setting people free is usually good at enslaving people too.

MARTIN [*not seriously*]: Yes, yes, yes, yes, yes –

GEORGIE: The trouble with you, Martin darling, is that you're always looking for a master.

MARTIN: No. Not now that I've got a beautiful mistress. [*He smiles at her, then they stare gravely at each other.*] Do you love me?

GEORGIE: Yes, to distraction. Do *you* love *me*?

MARTIN: Yes, infinitely.

GEORGIE [*very drily*]: Not infinitely. Let's be exact. Your love is a great but finite quantity.

[MARTIN *does not reply but shows by a deprecating gesture that he has understood her.*]

MARTIN: Do you want me to put my hand in the fire? [*He is standing looking down at her. She suddenly prostrates herself, her head at his feet. For a moment, a little too calmly, he accepts her homage. Then he kneels and embraces her. They kiss, then light cigarettes.*]

GEORGIE [*half playful, half serious*]: No! You know the things I want – nothing to do with hands in fires. I want to meet your brother. I want to go to New York with you.

MARTIN: Well, you're *not* going to meet my brother, but we *will* go to New York. I'm sorry I lost my nerve about it, last time. We will go. Only for God's sake stop talking about paying your own fare. You might at least let me spend my profits on something that gives me pleasure.

GEORGIE: The trouble is, I just can't imagine you making profits and being a business man. You're far too clever. You ought to have been a don.

MARTIN [*laughing, yet rather irritated*]: For the fiftieth time
– certainly not. You seem to imagine that being a
don is the only proper way of being clever. [*He picks
up a pair of blue stockings and gives them to her.*] These are
meant to be worn, girl, to show off your pretty legs.
You haven't to turn into one of them.

GEORGIE [*beginning to put them on, stubbornly*]: You got the
best History First of your year, didn't you?

MARTIN: Certainly. But I also inherited one of the sound-
est little family businesses in S.W.1 – just having a
try in Hocks and Moselles – dependable in Burgund-
ies – noble in clarets – as you ought to know by this
time –

GEORGIE: What did Alexander get, by the way?

MARTIN: You never give up, do you, angel? My dear
brother, in his days of youth and promise, got a *Prix
de Rome*, rather better than our Firsts, I imagine. But
like Rosemary, he draws an income out of the business, and unlike Rosemary, he's damned lazy. Alexander would probably have been a better sculptor if
he'd never had a penny.

GEORGIE: Perhaps all those girls of yours have done him
in – I mean, the girls you said you passed on to him
because he couldn't get any of his own –

MARTIN: Maybe. But I'm certainly not going to pass
you on.

GEORGIE: Meeting him isn't being passed on – I hope.
[*She has now finished putting her stockings on. He is wandering around, idly tidying up here and there. After a pause,
she continues casually.*]

GEORGIE: *She* know your brother.

MARTIN: Who does?

GEORGIE: Palmer Anderson's half-sister – Honor Klein.

MARTIN: I know. They met on some committee or other

at the time of the Mexican Art Exhibition. I saw her myself at that show – somebody pointed her out. The Female Don in person. Why do those women have to look like that?

GEORGIE: Those women! Darling dear, I'm one of those women now. [*She pulls her hair back behind her ears with an air of mock austerity.*]

MARTIN: *You* don't look as if you'd been dug out of remote desert sands.

GEORGIE: Well, she's spent a lot of time in weird places – living with tribes – after all, she's an anthropologist. But you talk about your Palmer having power in him. Sister Honor *really* has. My God – she used to terrify me.

MARTIN: Why? Because you don't look like something in a museum, it doesn't mean you're not as good as she is.

GEORGIE: Me? I'm not in that class. I don't carry half as many guns.

[GEORGIE, *who has been dressing herself, has now pulled on an unusual red chequered scarf.*]

What's the matter, darling?

MARTIN: You don't seem to like your presents.

GEORGIE: I do like my presents. Why do you say that?

MARTIN [*not entirely serious, but not playful*]: That scarf you're wearing! Have you forgotten already I've just given you a heavenly new one for Christmas? You know how jealous I am. That scarf's before my time. It's a prehistoric scarf. [*As she tries to interrupt.*] I know – I know – just habit, putting that thing on. But don't forget I'm still here. Be tactful if you can't be loving.

GEORGIE: Oh – Martin – it's all this hurrying in and out, this hateful having-to-go, that makes you say things

like that. You know I'm loving. I'm so loving I don't
have to be tactful. You know I adore my presents.
[*She rises, taking the scarf off, and looks at him. He returns
her look, smiles and holds her arms lightly.*]

MARTIN: It's all right, angel. Tell me what you'll be
doing on Christmas Day. I shall want to think about
you.

GEORGIE [*frowning*]: Oh – I shall be out with some of the
chaps. There's a big party on – for some of us home-
less types. [*Pause.*] I won't want to think about you.
It's odd how much it hurts at these times, not being
part of your proper family. At Christmas it hurts,
somehow, specially.

MARTIN [*chattily, avoding the intense*]: I'll be having just a
quiet day with Antonia. We're staying in London this
time.

GEORGIE [*hastily*]: I don't want to know. I don't want to
know what you do when you're not with me. It's
better not to feed the imagination. I prefer to think
that when you aren't here you don't exist.

[*They gaze at each other.*]

MARTIN: I'm bloody lucky.

GEORGIE: You mean you're bloody safe. Oh, you're safe
all right, damn you.

MARTIN: *Liaison dangereuse.* Yet we lie, somehow, out of
danger.

GEORGIE [*breaking away, not violently*]: *You* do. If Antonia
ever found out about this you'd drop me like a hot
potato.

MARTIN [*laughing, taking it lightly*]: Nonsense, nonsense!
She won't find out. And if she did, I'd manage. You're
essential to me, my dear child.

GEORGIE: No-one's *essential* to anyone. There you go –
looking at your watch again. All right – all right – go

if you must – go, go, go. What about one for the road?
Shall I open the claret?

MARTIN: Georgie – how many times must I tell you
never to drink claret unless it's been open at least two
hours?

GEORGIE: Don't be so holy about it. As far as I'm concerned the stuff is just booze.

MARTIN: Little barbarian! Now I really must go.

GEORGIE: When'll I see you?

MARTIN: Not till after Christmas. Twenty-eighth –
twenty-ninth perhaps. But I'll ring up before that
anyway.

[MARTIN *has pushed up the sleeve of her jersey and is stroking
her arm.*]

Wonderful stuff – flesh.

GEORGIE: Mmmm. [*A pause.*] I wonder if we'll ever be
able to be more open about this thing? I do rather
hate the bloody lies. [*As Martin is silent.*] Well – I
suppose not.

MARTIN: We're stuck with the bloody lies, I'm afraid,
my dear. [*Pause.*] And yet – you know this may sound
perverse, but it's part of the nature, it's almost part
of the charm, of this relationship of ours – its being
so utterly private.

GEORGIE: Very perverse, I'd say. You mean it's something essentially clandestine, and that if it was ever
exposed to the light of day it would crumble to pieces?
I don't think I like that idea.

MARTIN [*rising and looking round for his overcoat*]: I didn't
quite say that, Georgie. But it is true that knowledge,
other people's knowledge, does modify what it touches. You remember the legend of Psyche. She was told
that if she revealed she was pregnant, her child would
be mortal. But if she kept it secret it would be a god.

GEORGIE [*as she helps him with his overcoat*]: You want something perfect, don't you, something beautiful – small, limited, but beautiful. Perhaps after all you're an artist, like your brother. [*She puts her hands on his shoulders, studying him.*]

MARTIN [*gentle, apologetic*]: If it has to be incomplete, it may as well be – beautiful.

GEORGIE: I could do with a little less beauty and a little more good old formless reality. But there. You'd better go, Martin, or I shall begin to torment you. Be off, my darling, my love. [*She pushes him towards door.*]

MARTIN: Now, now, say goodbye properly. [*He kisses her.*] Don't forget I love you.

GEORGIE: I'm not likely to forget that. Anything else, dear?

MARTIN: And – well – happy Christmas, Georgie.

GEORGIE [*laughing rather harshly*]: Oh yes, of course – happy Christmas! Merry Christmas! Happy Christmas!

[*She pushes him out of the door, then blows out the candles, draws the curtain and kneels on the bed to look out of the window, to catch a glimpse of him below. A neon sign across the street winks above her head. She throws herself upon the bed, and sobs quietly as the scene fades out.*]

SCENE II

The drawing room in the Lynch-Gibbons' house at Hereford Square, an hour later. A lavish, elegant panelled room, finely furnished but comfortable. A large number of expensive Christmas cards are set out on the piano. A bright fire glows in the grate.

ANTONIA *enters and switches on more light. She is a very handsome and rather voluptuous woman of forty-six, tall and well-dressed, with big tawny intelligent eyes and a mobile ex-*

pressive mouth. She wears her long goldenish hair in a bun. She is obviously agitated and restless. She crosses and calls off.

ANTONIA [*calling*]: Martin. Martin.

MARTIN (*a vague shout from another part of the house*): I'm up here.

[ANTONIA *moves restlessly, pours out a drink but does not touch it. After a few moments* MARTIN *enters wearing a dressing gown and scarf. His manner is not really easy with her.*]

MARTIN: Hello, darling. You're late, you bad girl. When you didn't turn up, I thought I'd have my bath. Let's have our drinks now, shall we?

[*She has retreated towards the door and leans against it, staring at him, while he goes to the drinks.*]

MARTIN: Oh – you've poured yourself something already. What is it?

ANTONIA: I don't know. I wasn't thinking –

MARTIN [*fiddling with the drinks*]: Better start again, hadn't we? Sherry – something with gin?

ANTONIA [*confusedly*]: Yes – if you like –

MARTIN: What? Which? Come on Antonia, don't be a wild bird this evening. Sherry, I think – um? [*He pours out two glasses.*] Now come and have your drink, my dearest, and tell me all about it.

[*He sits at one end of the sofa and holds out her drink. She comes across gingerly and takes the drink, sitting at the other end of the sofa, as he stares at her and continues talking.*]

What is it, darling? Did your analysis take a new and ugly turn?

[*He reaches a hand towards her but she shrinks back. He speaks more sharply.*]

What's the matter, Antonia? Has something bad happened?

ANTONIA [*confused, emotional*]: Yes. Well, no, not really.

17

Wait a minute. Sorry. [*She sips her drink, then pours the rest into his glass.*]

MARTIN: For God's sake, darling. What it it? What's happened?

ANTONIA [*urgently*]: It's this. I've got to tell you now. There's a sort of – of *necessity* about telling you now. That makes it easier for me, perhaps. There's no way of breaking it gently. Martin darling – it's about me and Palmer.

MARTIN [*smiling*]: What about you and Palmer, angel?

ANTONIA: Well – just that. Just that – *just that*.

MARTIN [*gently*]: If you mean you're a bit in love with him, I'm not surprised. In a way I'm a bit in love with him myself.

ANTONIA: Don't be flippant, Martin. This is serious. It's *fatal*.

[*He pushes back the hair from her brow. She becomes rigid, closing her eyes.*]

MARTIN: Well, do stop looking like that, dearest. As if you were going to be shot. Calm down and have your drink. [*As she shakes her head.*] Well, talk to me rationally and don't frighten me out of my wits.

ANTONIA [*with a kind of desperate monotony*]: You see, it's not a matter of being a bit in love. It's a matter of being very desperately and deeply in love. Perhaps we ought to have told you sooner, only it seemed so improbable, so impossible, such an extreme love. But now we're – quite certain.

MARTIN: Look, darling, this sort of thing often happens in analysis. Transference, you know. Need we be quite so solemn about it?

ANTONIA [*cutting in sharply*]: Don't be stupid. This has nothing to do with his work. We both feel the same. And now that I *know*, you see, I want a divorce.

MARTIN [*rising*]: Nonsense! Now please stop saying wild things you don't mean.

ANTONIA [*urgently*]: Martin, please help me. I do mean it and it will save us a lot of pain if you'll understand me *now* and see what things are like *now*. Please try – please.

MARTIN: You're in an over-excited state, my sweet – has Palmer been giving you drugs?

ANTONIA: No, no, *no*. I hate talking like this but I *must*. I want a divorce, Martin. I'm deeply, deeply in love. Just believe me and then let me go away. I know it's absurd, I know it's dreadful, but I'm in love and I'm absolutely relentless.

MARTIN: All right, you are. Well, if you're so much in love with your analyst perhaps you'd better go to bed with him. Only don't talk nonsense to me about divorce for I simply won't listen.

ANTONIA [*in small toneless voice*]: I've already been to bed with him.

MARTIN: My God! [*He pulls her to her feet and holds her.*] Since when? and how many times?

ANTONIA [*afraid of him, but firm*]: That doesn't matter. If you really want the details I'll tell you later. Now I just want to tell you the main truth, to tell you that you've got to set me free. This thing has overwhelmed me, Martin. Honestly, it's all or nothing.

MARTIN [*releasing her, drier now*]: Well, let me recommend *nothing*.

ANTONIA: Oh darling, I hate this, I do. You've been so perfect to me. But I'm beyond any thoughts about justification. I'm just desperate.

MARTIN: Yes, I have been perfect, haven't I? And remember, we've been happy. I want to go on being happy.

ANTONIA: Happy – yes, I suppose so. But happiness isn't the point. You know as well as I do we aren't getting anywhere.

MARTIN: One doesn't have to get anywhere in a marriage. It's not a public conveyance.

ANTONIA: You must face the fact that you're a disappointed man.

MARTIN: I'm damned if I'm a disappointed man. What you mean is that you're a disappointed woman – though God knows why.

ANTONIA: A marriage is an adventure in development, and ours is at a standstill. I was conscious of that even before I fell in love with Palmer. I'm only a little older than you, of course, but being so much more mature, I've had to be a sort of mother to you. I've prevented you from growing up – from reaching maturity – full integration –

MARTIN: Spare me the clinical stuff, for God's sake. Leave me because you want someone else, let's have honest lust, not pseudo-science. But in any case, you aren't going, I won't let you. I want to go on being married to you, so if you must keep jumping into bed with him, you'd better resign yourself to having a husband *and* a lover.

ANTONIA: No. No. I must go to him, Martin, I've got to. I'm going *now*, literally tonight, as soon as I've packed some things. [*Pause.*] I'm extremely grateful to you for being so rational about it.

MARTIN: I'm not being rational. I can hear what you say, Antonia, but your words make no more sense to me than if you were a madwoman.

ANTONIA: Listen, darling – *please*! We'll go together as soon as I've got my things, and then you can talk to Palmer –

MARTIN: Certainly not. It's the most tasteless repulsive idea I've ever heard of. I refuse to be a cuckold going to be measured for his horns!

ANTONIA: You know it's not like that at all, dearest. So do be gentle with Palmer. Just try to imagine how miserable he's been about this business. You know how terribly attached to you he is.

MARTIN: To hell with his attachments! I will *not* go and see him. He would say we must behave like civilised people while I'd be wanting to kick his teeth in.

ANTONIA: He's expecting you, darling.

MARTIN: Antonia, let me out of this bad dream. *This* is what is real – *this*, our marriage.

[ANTONIA, *beginning now to be tearful, shakes her head. He goes to her.*]

Anyway, my darling, my Antonia, what would I ever do without you?

[*He puts his arms around her. She cries a little, then peeps at him, smiling through tears.*]

ANTONIA [*softly*]: I knew you'd be good about it, darling. I knew you'd be very good about it. I'm so relieved to have told you. I did hate lying, deceiving you. Thank you. Thank you.

MARTIN: What am I being thanked for?

ANTONIA: Ah my dear – I love you. You know, you know you need never do without me. [*Pause.*] And now if you'll wait – I shan't be long – ten minutes, quarter of an hour, just time for you to have another drink and finish dressing – we'll go and see Palmer.

MARTIN: No!

ANTONIA: Ah – my dear. Please. Yes. [*She embraces him.*]

MARTIN: No!

ANTONIA: Yes. My child. My dear child.

[*She backs out slowly, keeping her gaze upon him. He stares after her, bewildered, almost stunned, and then like a sleep-walker pours himself out a drink and begins sipping it, blank-eyed.*]

SCENE III

Palmer Anderson's study, an hour later. It is a large, bright, hygienic room, decorated and furnished in a sleek modern style. There is a large desk and a black leather couch. Various Oriental objects are prominent.

After a moment or two MARTIN *enters, wearing an overcoat and no hat, looking rather vague and untidy. He stares about.*

PALMER *materialises from the back of the room. He is a man of over fifty, half American, tall and lean with a well-preserved boyishness. His small round head is covered with soft close-cropped silver-grey hair, and his face has a smooth, formidably clean look. He is well-dressed in a thin light-weight suit.*

PALMER: You found a parking space?

MARTIN: Yes.

PALMER: Good. Antonia will join us shortly.

MARTIN: Damned hot in here.

PALMER: Well, take that coat off, my dear Martin –

MARTIN: Not yet. Perhaps not at all.

PALMER [*softly and slowly*]: You don't hate me, do you, Martin?

MARTIN: No, I don't hate you, Palmer.

PALMER: We are civilised people. We must try to be very lucid and very honest. We are civilised and intelligent people.

MARTIN: Yes. [*Pause.*] Antonia and I have been very happy. I hope she hasn't misled you here.

PALMER: Antonia could not mislead me if she tried.

Happiness, my dear Martin, is neither here nor there. Some people – and Antonia is one – conceive of their lives as a progress. Hers has been standing still for too long. She is due to move on.

MARTIN: You talk as if you were a policeman and she was a lorry –

PALMER: I put it badly –

MARTIN: You mean that 'marriage is an adventure in development'.

PALMER: Precisely.

MARTIN: So if Antonia has not been 'developing' – the whole thing acquires a sort of inevitability.

PALMER: Martin, I admire your capacity for facing facts. Yes, a sort of inevitability. In this admission there is no evasion of responsibility – on my part or on hers. There is no point in talking about guilt. Such talk would be insincere, whether in your accusations or in my confessions. But of course we are causing hurt and damage. For instance – to Antonia's mother –

MARTIN [*cutting in*]: Damn Antonia's mother! What about me?

PALMER: *You* will not be damaged, my dear Martin. [*He pauses and comes closer, regarding Martin with an air of tender consideration. Very smoothly.*] This is a big thing, Martin, something bigger than ourselves, something that holds us – all three.

MARTIN: Isn't it enough to have seduced one of us?

PALMER: Don't be crude, Martin. You'll see what I mean. I know Antonia very well, Martin. Better in some ways than you do. That's not your fault but my profession. I know *you* better in some ways than you do.

MARTIN: I doubt that. I've never subscribed to your

religion. But does it tell you we're all going to be better off?

PALMER: Yes. I don't say happier – though that's possible – but we'll *grow*, Martin, we'll *grow*. You've been a child to Antonia and she a mother to you, and that has kept you both spiritually speaking at a standstill. But you *will* grow up, you *will* change, more than may now seem to you possible. Haven't you sometimes realised the extent to which you now regard yourself both as a child and as an old man?

MARTIN [*obviously fighting this insight*]: No. Certainly not. Nonsense, nonsense. I reject your explanations.

PALMER: There you are, Martin.

MARTIN [*dabbing his face with a handkerchief*]: I wish you wouldn't keep repeating my name. You aren't hypnotising me, are you?

PALMER: Of course not. Relax, Martin. Look – you're streaming with perspiration. Let me take that coat [*as he takes off the overcoat*]. It's an important fact in this situation, of course, that there already exists between us a sincere deep relationship. You are certain you are not angry with me?

MARTIN: *Cher maitre!*

[PALMER, *the overcoat over his arm now, steers* MARTIN *to the couch on to which he sinks rather helplessly, while* PALMER *puts the neatly folded coat on a chair.*]

MARTIN: I'm much too hot. And I seem to have drunk too much already this evening. I feel dreadfully hurt, wounded, run over, confused, everything *but* angry.

PALMER [*smiling*]: You see, Martin, I'm wrapping nothing up.

MARTIN: Yes, you are. But very cleverly. I suspect it's all wrapping. You're too clever for me, Palmer.

PALMER: I knew you'd take it well, I knew you'd take it – splendidly –

MARTIN: You don't know yet how I'm taking it. Neither do I.

PALMER [*smiling*]: My dear fellow, your sense of humour will be the saving of us all. [*Closer, portentous.*] You see, it is not at all our idea that you should leave us. In a strange and rather wonderful way we can't do without you. We shall hold on to you, we shall look after you. You'll see.

MARTIN: I thought I was supposed to grow up.

PALMER: Oh – don't imagine it will be easy. But your liking me so much is the important thing.

MARTIN: How do you know I'll go on liking you, Palmer?

PALMER [*softly*]: *You will.*

[PALMER *smiles,* MARTIN *looks dubious. Enter* ANTONIA. *She looks enquiringly at Palmer, who signals to her that all is well.*]

MARTIN [*rising with difficulty*]: All three of us. Mmmm.

ANTONIA [*ecstatically*]: All three of us! [*Then, to* MARTIN.] I can't tell you how much it relieves and gladdens my heart to see you two dear beings at peace together.

MARTIN [*not unpleasantly*]: We're not. Palmer has just performed some conjuring trick.

ANTONIA: A good, good trick.

MARTIN: If a trick, not good. However, I don't seem to want to strangle either of you. I wonder why.

PALMER: There are reasons, Martin. Beautiful reasons.

MARTIN: Well, for God's sake don't tell me what they are.

ANTONIA [*enthusiastically*]: My dear, you have no notion how deeply, deeply good you are.

MARTIN: I'm beginning to realise. For one thing, it hurts so much.

ANTONIA: We won't let go of you.

PALMER: We'll never let go of you.

MARTIN: You can't have everything, you two.

ANTONIA: We can try, dearest Martin, we can try!

[*She draws the two men together. She kisses* MARTIN *on the cheek, and then, still holding him, turns to kiss* PALMER. *She is still holding them both, smiling from one to the other, when* HONOR KLEIN *enters quietly. She is a sturdily-built woman of about forty, with dark hair and complexion, and a heavy clever Jewish face. She is not wearing a hat but otherwise is sensibly dressed for travel on a cold day. She is carrying a bulky hold-all. She stares sardonically at the entwined trio for a moment or two. Then she kicks the door shut.*]

PALMER [*startled*]: Honor!

[*They have all sprung apart now.*]

I wasn't expecting you so early. Honor – Antonia is – here.

[ANTONIA *smiles, rather flustered.*]

And this is Martin Lynch-Gibbon – [*to Martin*] Have you met my sister?

HONOR [*ironically*]: I am very pleased to meet Mr. and Mrs. Lynch-Gibbon. I had not expected – quite this – party. [*She joins* ANTONIA, PALMER *and* MARTIN *together with a slight ironical gesture and a scornful glance at* MARTIN.]

MARTIN [*upset, bows*]: Dr. Klein. The party is over. I won't continue to intrude on this – family gathering. [*He joins* PALMER, ANTONIA *and* HONOR *together with an answering gesture and departs. They eye each other as the door bangs.*]

ACT ONE

SCENE IV

The Lynch-Gibbons' drawing room, early evening, the next day. MARTIN *ushers* ROSEMARY *in. He has been out himself, and has met her on the doorstep. He has had one or two drinks, and carries a bottle of whisky.* ROSEMARY *is carrying a great many odds and ends of parcels. She is thirty-seven, a bright, helpful, bird-like spinster, with small precise features and a prim voice.*

MARTIN [*as they enter*]: I'm so sorry you had to wait, flower. I've been at the pub. I seem to live there these days.

ROSEMARY: What I really wanted to make sure of, dear, is that you'd come to me for Christmas Day. Alexander's coming, though he pretends not to like Christmas. So there'd be the three of us – almost like old times. You will come, won't you, Martin dear? [*As* MARTIN *hesitates.*] Don't tell me you've promised to spend the day with *them*.

MARTIN: Antonia and Palmer? No. I think they may be staying at some country hotel over Christmas.

ROSEMARY: I'm not surprised. Antonia always did adore hotels – and of course he's an American.

MARTIN: All right, flower – I'll be with you, and thank you for asking me. You and I and Alexander will eat too much and then get quietly plastered.

ROSEMARY: Poor Martin – I don't know *what* to say – *what* to think. I'm sorry of course – I mean, after so many years and everybody thinking it such a splendid marriage. But in another way I can't help feeling, well, sort of relieved. I never did quite get on with Antonia. Though, of course, I pretended to for your

27

sake. And I'm not surprised it's an American psycho-analyst – especially a rich one who doesn't have to work too hard – I regard that as *typical*.

MARTIN: I'm not with you, flower. Typical of *what*?

ROSEMARY: Well, really it's the equivalent now of all that running off with violinists and actors Mother used to talk about. Antonia's the *type*. Just as she is about clothes – *and* hotels. You know what I mean, darling.

MARTIN [*not angrily*]: I'm not sure that I do, but let's drop the subject. Drink? Cigarette?

ROSEMARY: No thank you, dear. Look, don't let Antonia cheat you about the furniture and things, will you? As she's the guilty party it should all really belong to you, you know.

MARTIN: Oh, we'll sort things out.

ROSEMARY: I think you're wonderful! You don't seem bitter at all. I should be mad with rage if I were you. You treated that man as your best friend.

MARTIN: He's still my best friend.

ROSEMARY: You're very philosophical – but don't over-do it, dear. A bit of good cursing may be just what you need. You must be miserable and bitter some-where inside.

MARTIN: I'm miserable everywhere inside. Bitterness is another thing. There's no point in it. Can we talk about something else, flower?

ROSEMARY: Where will you live now?

MARTIN: Here. It's my house and I still like it.

ROSEMARY: But don't you think you ought to get a flat now? It's not easy of course, and you may have to pay the earth, but I'll help – I love finding flats. Don't you think something small and cosy – near the Bromp-ton Road – ?

MARTIN: God forbid! I'd rather stay here even if it all goes to cobwebs, rats and ruin.

ROSEMARY: Don't be silly, dear. You sound like Miss Thing in What's-it – *Great Expectations*. And don't you think you'd feel better if we put up some Christmas decorations? You can have some of mine – silver stars and chains – they're in one of these parcels –

MARTIN [*as she threatens to undo the parcel*]: No, no. No, no, no. I'll enjoy them all the more when I see them at your place.

ROSEMARY: Dear Martin, Alexander and I will stand by you.

MARTIN: Yes, thanks. Where is he, by the way?

ROSEMARY: He's gone to some gallery to pick up a head. Oh, and, Martin, just before you see him – you know he's dreadfully cut up about you and Antonia.

MARTIN: Naturally. He adores Antonia.

ROSEMARY: I happened to be there when he opened her letter. And do you know he looked really *shaken*.

MARTIN [*surprised and irritated*]: Her letter? So she wrote to him about it, did she? Charming! Now he's got both sides of the picture!

ROSEMARY: Well, I gather so. Anyway all I'm saying is do be kind and tactful with him, not sort of casual – please, Martin.

MARTIN: To console him for my wife having left me? All right, flower.

ROSEMARY: Martin! You really are! [*She begins giggling. The front door bell rings.*] That'll be Alexander. I'll let him in – and then I must get on with my decorations – I've got awfully behind with the kissing bough this year. Come about half-past twelve, dear.

[*She gives him a sisterly peck and hurries out.* MARTIN *pours himself a drink. Then enter* ALEXANDER *carrying a large*

crate, which he puts down. He is forty-five, and dresses in an
unconventional dandified manner. He resembles MARTIN, *but*
looks, attractively, a shade more degenerate. He has the sort of
face which is called 'noble' when it belongs to an animal.]

ALEXANDER: Martin! My poor dear fellow.

MARTIN: Alexander! Have a drink. Sherry – gin – whiskey?

ALEXANDER: Whiskey – straight, please.

MARTIN: You got my letter? I just couldn't say it all on the telephone.

ALEXANDER: I don't think you said it all in the letter, did you?

MARTIN: Enough.

ALEXANDER: Did you get anything more out of Palmer? Did he tell you anything else?

MARTIN: I didn't ask him.

ALEXANDER: You seem to have taken it very clamly.

MARTIN: Oh yes – very.

ALEXANDER: I don't say I would have sprung upon him like a wild animal, but I'd have felt I'd a right to know some details –

MARTIN: And very charming they'd have been, wouldn't they?

ALEXANDER: No, not that kind of thing. But I'd have wanted to understand.

MARTIN: Oh – I *understand.* You must remember I've been pretty close to Palmer, and this makes it impossible to ask, but also makes it unnecessary.

ALEXANDER: And Antonia seems happy?

MARTIN: It's the beatific vision.

ALEXANDER: Why – for God's sake?

MARTIN: You mean, you don't like him.

ALEXANDER: I never did. He's an imitation human

being: beautifully finished, exquisitely coloured, but imitation.

MARTIN: He's a magician, and that can inspire dislike. But he's warm-blooded. He needs love, just like anybody else. I can't help being touched by the way he's tried to *hold on* to me, as well as Antonia, in this curious business.

ALEXANDER: Watch it, brother. In real life magicians can be dangerous.

MARTIN: Antonia wrote to you, Rosemary says.

ALEXANDER [*uneasy*]: Yes, yes . . . I was stunned by her letter.

MARTIN: But surely you didn't get it before I telephoned? She would hardly have written to you before she even told me!

ALEXANDER: No, no – of course not. But I simply didn't take it in when you rang. I couldn't believe it. Her letter convinced me. And yours, of course. What are your plans now?

MARTIN: Oh, business as usual, I suppose.

ALEXANDER: Why not come down and live in the country with us?

MARTIN: What would I do there?

ALEXANDER: Nothing.

MARTIN: Come!

ALEXANDER: Why not? You could fleet the time away. It's the earthly paradise, as we all saw with perfect clarity in childhood before we were corrupted by the world. If you insisted on occupation I would teach you how to model in clay or carve snakes and weasels out of tree roots. The trouble with people nowadays is they don't know how to do nothing. I've had quite a job teaching Rosemary, and she's certainly more gifted in that direction than you are.

MARTIN: You are an artist, and for you doing nothing is doing something. No. When I've pulled myself together a bit I'll try to get some writing done. Antonia was – time-consuming.

ALEXANDER [*murmurs*]: Beautifully. [*He warms himself at the fire.*]

> 'Since I left Plumtree
>
> Down in Tennessee
>
> It's the first time I've been warm.'

MARTIN: Show me some of the results of your inactivity. [ALEXANDER *opens the crate and takes out a bronze head which he places on a stool.*]

ALEXANDER: Know who this is? [*He turns a light on to the head.*]

MARTIN: Good God – Antonia. I haven't seen that one in years. But it can't be her without the body . . .

ALEXANDER: Yes, some people *are* more their body than others. All the same, heads are us most of all; they are the apex of our incarnation. The best thing about being God would be making the heads.

MARTIN: I don't think I like a sculpted head alone. It seems to represent an unfair advantage, a sort of illicit and incomplete relationship.

ALEXANDER: An illicit and incomplete relationship. Yes. Perhaps an obsession. Freud on Medusa. The head can represent the female genitals, feared not desired.

MARTIN: I didn't mean anything so fancy. Any savage likes to collect heads.

ALEXANDER: You wouldn't let me collect yours! [*He draws his hand down over the back of* MARTIN'S *head.*] You never let me sculpt you. . . .

MARTIN: Certainly not. You're a magician too, you know. You gain power over people by making images of them. [*He contemplates Antonia's head a moment longer, then shivers, and turns away.*] All the same I envy you. You have a *technique* for finding out more about what's real. Any artist has.

ALEXANDER: Any man has. It's called morality.

MARTIN: Out of practice. I'm a novice at reality. I've been living in a dream world of love.

ALEXANDER [*wanders to the window and draws back the curtain*]: Funny, it's still light outside. [*He switches off the lights and looks out into the yellowish twilight.*] Stopped snowing. There's a blackbird on the path. How very black he looks.

> 'The ousel-cock so black of hue
> With orange-tawny bill.'

MARTIN: You quote but too aptly, brother.

ALEXANDER: *Too* aptly?

MARTIN: You don't recall the rest?

ALEXANDER: No.

MARTIN: 'The throstle with his note so true,
> The wren with little quill,
> The finch, the sparrow, and the lark,
> The plain-song cuckoo gray,
> Whose note full many a man doth mark,
> And dare not answer nay.'

[*After a moment's silence carol singers are heard far away. Their carol is 'Once in Royal David's City'.*]

ALEXANDER [*hesitantly*]: There's a question I've been wanting to ask you – but you might not like it.

MARTIN: Well?

ALEXANDER: Have you ever been unfaithful to Antonia?

MARTIN: No – of course I haven't –

[*The lights fade out on them and come up on* GEORGIE's ROOM. GEORGIE *is sitting on her bed reading a letter. Martin's voice is heard speaking its contents.*]

MARTIN [*voice only*]: My darling Georgie, I have not

spent Christmas quite as I expected. On the evening when I last saw you Antonia suddenly announced that she wished to leave me and get married to Palmer Anderson. As you may imagine, I am suffering from shock. Indeed I feel scarcely sane and nothing seems solid or real any more. Darling child, your love and your devotion have been so precious to me: support me now with patience. Excuse this cowardly and distracted letter. Your poor discredited prince kisses your feet. Hope and fear nothing if you can. Please bear with me and *go on loving me.* I'll come soon – not at once, but soon. Martin.

SCENE V

Palmer's Study, the next day. Enter ANTONIA *and* MARTIN

ANTONIA: Darling, I'm so glad you could come. Palmer wanted so terribly to talk to you again. I think he feels he can – help you.

MARTIN: It's very kind of him, especially when he has so many other things to think about.

ANTONIA: Whatever would he be thinking about, what would either of us be thinking about, but you? We think of nothing else.

MARTIN: Decent of you.

ANTONIA: Please, darling, don't do that.

MARTIN: Don't do what, for Christ's sake?

ANTONIA: Be sort of blank and sarcastic. And please, if you can, be nice to Palmer. He's so terribly worried about what you feel about him and so terribly anxious to please you. You could hurt him dreadfully by the smallest thing.

34

MARTIN: I'm not being blank and sarcastic. But I do wish everyone would stop scheming for my welfare. I'm perfectly well able to look after myself.

ANTONIA: But we want to look after you! [*She comes closer to him and lays her hand on his arm.*]

MARTIN [*suddenly rigid with emotion*]: No, Antonia.

ANTONIA: Yes, Martin. Don't flee from me. We must still be able to touch each other.

MARTIN: Does your psychoanalyst advise this?

ANTONIA: Please! You mustn't say these bitter things.

MARTIN: I should have thought that was pretty mild. But then I seem to have set myself such a high standard. I suppose I shall have to keep it up now.

ANTONIA: Yes, yes, you will have to keep it up, won't you! [*She laughs with relief.*] Ah, you are generous, my dear. Well, I must go and pack. Palmer and I are off to the country this afternoon. I thought the change would do him good, he's *so* overtired. And, honestly, it's all a bit awkward here with Honor brooding about the house all the time. Don't hurry away, do stay and have a nice long talk with Palmer. It must be – so cold – over there.

MARTIN: Yes. [*Moved.*] You've got a new dress.

ANTONIA: Ah –

[*She stretches out a hand, and they touch finger tips. She goes. MARTIN looks after her.*

Enter PALMER.]

MARTIN: Sir, you whistled. I have come.

PALMER: No, no, this is all wrong, all wrong.

MARTIN: What is?

PALMER: Your attitude, your vision of where we stand. You must forgive me for being such a perfectionist. If I tell you a few true things you won't, will you, think that I'm being bossy?

MARTIN: One doesn't think of gods and angels as being bossy.

PALMER: There you go again, wrong again. You conceal your anger behind this sort of ridiculous fawning. But neither of these things will do us any good at all. No, no, let me take the penitential place this time.

[*He lies on the couch. Throughout the scene, as* MARTIN *moves,* PALMER *contorts himself gracefully, like an Indian god.*]

MARTIN: You might be thankful that my anger is at least restrained by what you charmingly call my fawning.

PALMER: Martin, Martin, don't you see where we are? Miles and miles beyond these conventional responses. [*Pause.*] I want to make you feel free.

MARTIN: Freedom is not a value for me, Palmer.

PALMER: There has always been a contest between us. A quite private contest which has nothing whatever to do with Antonia. And if we wrestle now, it is you who must play the angel. [*Pause.*] You see you mustn't, as it were, muff it.

MARTIN: Muff what, for heaven's sake?

PALMER: Your suffering.

MARTIN: That! I think at least my suffering is my own affair. [*Pause.*] What do you want me to do with it, anyway? Am I to suffer or not to suffer, to show it or not to show it? To punish you or not to punish you?

PALMER: Precisely. As for suffering, you can't choose. As for showing it, of course you must show it. For our punishment, which was the third thing you spoke of.

MARTIN: Yes, you are a perfectionist.

PALMER: You see, that *is* our punishment, that you suffer most and that you suffer at our hands. That is what makes us – your victims, your slaves.

MARTIN: This is metaphysics, Palmer.

PALMER: No. Psychology. You simply dare not *look* at Antonia and me at present. It hurts too much. So you remain in a state of illusion which you express by treating us on the surface too well and underneath too badly.

MARTIN: What do you want, then?

PALMER: Justice, Martin. To be seen as we really are.

MARTIN: You are an old word-player, aren't you?

PALMER: Martin, I speak most sincerely out of the most desperate need. Only your act of justice will restore us all – to freedom, to the real world. Don't you see?

MARTIN: So I have to play the part of the redeemer as well.

PALMER: You may find that you hate us – at first. But if you shirk nothing, if you avoid all illusion and all consolation, and if you keep on really *looking* at us – you will come, in the end –

MARTIN: To love you?

PALMER: Only love will serve our turn here. A very, very rare thing – though no name is taken oftener in vain.

MARTIN: So I'm to license your lower sort with my higher sort?

PALMER: You choose to jest. But you understand me all the same. You must go right through with it, Martin. And my punishment will be that I cannot go with you.

MARTIN: The gods can't suffer.

PALMER: If the gods can't suffer that is their punishment. And that is why they have to create us. But I am no god, Martin. See. I am abject. Prostrate. At your feet.

MARTIN [*exclaiming, trying to break the spell*]: You always *muddle* me so, Palmer.

PALMER: Please.

MARTIN: I don't even know what you're asking of me. But all right. You're the expert. You're the sage. Have it your own way. See it your own way. All right, all right.

PALMER: Thank you. Yes. You are – generous. You are – just. You have made me happy – so happy I could almost fall asleep now.

[*He seems to sleep for a moment.* MARTIN *stares at him and then makes a confused gesture.* PALMER *gets up.*]

Did I sleep? For a second I think I did. Now I must go and fetch Antonia. Stay here a while, Martin. Fix yourself a drink. And thank you, thank you.

[PALMER *goes.* MARTIN *stands dazed and bewildered. Then he pours himself a drink. Enter* HONOR KLEIN.]

MARTIN: I'm so sorry. I – er – Palmer left me here. May I give you a drink?

HONOR: No, thank you. [*She moves to the bookcase and speaks with her back to him.*] Mr. Lynch-Gibbon, may I ask you what *you* think about it?

MARTIN: About – what, Dr. Klein?

HONOR: You know quite well what I mean. Do you think they are doing the right thing?

MARTIN: Do you mean – morally?

HONOR: No, not *morally* – I mean for their life.

MARTIN: Yes, I do think they are doing the right thing.

HONOR [*turning to face him*]: I wonder if you realise that you are being very bad for them?

MARTIN: No. I'm inclined to think I'm being rather good for them, if anything.

HONOR: Do you believe you are acting well?

MARTIN: I certainly don't believe I am acting badly. Do you imagine I enjoy this?

HONOR: I don't know what you *enjoy*, Mr. Lynch-Gibbon. I only see what you do. I wonder if you realise how easily you could get your wife back?

MARTIN: I'm afraid you are mistaken, Dr. Klein. I am entirely without power.

HONOR: I don't say you ought to have beaten your wife and kicked my brother downstairs, but there was no need positively to push them into each others' arms.

MARTIN: I assure you, they are both self-moving and quite independent of me. And if I choose to behave in a civilised manner I think that's my affair. And now if you'll excuse me –

HONOR: They are not independent of you, as you perfectly well know.

MARTIN: Well, if they choose to depend a little on my – generosity – that does them credit.

HONOR: Your generosity, Mr. Lynch-Gibbon, seems to me a rather dubious piece of self-indulgence. As for those two, they are something in your dream. You maintain their world in existence, they depend on you, on your gaze, on your credence.

MARTIN: You are perhaps no philosopher, Dr. Klein. A dream which endures is not a dream. If they can be happy together, with or without my assistance, good luck to them.

HONOR: There is such a thing as living in untruth, and even if it lasts a lifetime it is still untruth. Your wife and my brother are both experts in self-deception. They have enchanted themselves into believing in this wholly ridiculous match. But they are only half enchanted. In order to complete the spell they need you, as an admiring spectator. They are only half enchanted and they are both of them terrified. If instead of prolonging this disastrous piece of idiocy you were to shake them out of it, which you could do in a moment, they'd both be profoundly relieved.

MARTIN: I'm sorry, but I just think you're wrong. Perhaps there is something I can do for them. But it's something to do with – enduring it all without resentment.

HONOR: Suffering for them with a loving heart?

MARTIN: If you like, yes.

HONOR: Mr. Lynch-Gibbon, you make me feel very sick indeed.

MARTIN: After all, I am in a position to know the truth about both of them.

HONOR: Truth! Truth was lost sight of long ago. In a matter like this you can't have both truth and what you call civilisation. Let me put it another way, Mr. Lynch-Gibbon. You are a violent man. You simply cannot get away with it.

MARTIN: Get away with what?

HONOR: This – intimacy with your wife's seducer.

MARTIN: I'm not one of your primitive savages, Dr. Klein. I don't believe in vendettas. I think the transference of violence from one place to another has got to end somewhere.

HONOR: The transference of violence from one place to another can only *end* in a saint. For the rest of us it is simply a question of the form in which we are to pass the violence on.

MARTIN: Well, if it comes to that, what's to stop me from being a saint, if I try?

[HONOR *simply looks at him.*]

All right, all right.

HONOR: You cannot cheat the dark gods, Mr. Lynch-Gibbon. Perhaps it is no business of mine if you choose to be as you say 'quite without power', and to abandon your wife when she needs you most. But everything in this life has to be paid for. You do my brother no good by letting him off. By this so-called civilised behaviour you are only sparing yourself, letting *yourself* off, because your proper task is too unpleasant. But sooner or later you will have to become a centaur and kick your way out.

MARTIN: I'm sorry. But I believe there is a much better way for all three of us.

HONOR: I don't think you really want your wife back at all.

MARTIN: You can hardly expect me to dispute with you about that.

HONOR: You are very long-suffering, Mr. Lynch-Gibbon. You must excuse my doubts about your saintliness. But only lies and evil come from letting people off.

MARTIN: I don't imagine that you ever let people off, do you, Dr. Klein?

HONOR [*smiling*]: No. With me people pay as they earn.

SCENE VI

Georgie Hands' lodging, early afternoon, three days later. GEORGIE *is working. Enter a subdued, distracted-looking* MARTIN. *They regard each other.*

GEORGIE [*gravely*]: Well, now you're in a fix, aren't you, you old double-dealer?

MARTIN [*gratefully*]: Georgie – angel! [*He presses her hand to his lips. Then, humbly for him.*] Yes, I am in a fix. But you'll be very kind to me, won't you? You'll let me off.

GEORGIE [*solemnly, rather sadly*]: I love you, Martin. You never seem to get this simple point into your old head.

MARTIN [*not entirely playful*]: *Old head* is right. I'm not sure it isn't cracked. I took it to the office this morning, hoping to keep it there all day, but after three hours nothing seemed real – buying wine – selling wine – absurd –

GEORGIE [*not too reproachfully*]: You've not changed the subject, have you?

MARTIN: No, my darling. [*A pause while he looks at her.*] You don't mind if we keep our thing secret still? I just can't cope, otherwise.

GEORGIE: I don't understand why. But – if you want to. For myself, I'd like to publish it in *The Times*.

MARTIN: It would hurt Antonia so much if she knew. [*He waits a moment for a reply to this and then, not getting one, hurries on.*] The least I can do is make things easy for her. The way we've managed it all is really rather an achievement, you know. I mean, without bitterness. I just don't want to add any more strains at present.

GEORGIE: This *without bitterness* idea seems to me rather obscene –

MARTIN: Georgie – come off it.

GEORGIE: I'm sorry but it does. And I suspect you of wanting to play the virtuous aggrieved husband –

MARTIN: Why should I?

GEORGIE: To keep Palmer and Antonia in your power.

MARTIN: In my power? No indeed, I'm in *their* power.

GEORGIE: I'm under-rating your goodness, am I, darling?

MARTIN: It's all much simpler. I just want to finish the thing off perfectly without any more complications. If Antonia *knew* she'd want long intimate talks about it, she'd want to *understand*. And I couldn't bear that. Don't you see, dearest little donkey?

GEORGIE [*as if with reservations*]: I do see – yes. [*She kneels by the fire.*] You speak of *the thing* – which has to be finished off perfectly – as if it were a sort of work of art. No real people involved. Sometimes I think you're a very odd fish, Martin, my darling. But of course I do see, yes, about the intimate talks. Promise you'll never have an intimate talk about me with Antonia?

MARTIN: I promise, dear darling, I do promise.

GEORGIE: Anyhow, don't worry. You don't have to *do* anything special, here I mean. It's only me.

MARTIN [*fervently*]: Thank God it's only you, and thank God *for* you. Dear Georgie, you absolutely save my sanity. I knew you would.

GEORGIE: Well, now stop looking so *tall*.

[MARTIN *kneels beside her and they embrace. For a few moments she gives herself up to this, but then checks both herself and him, gently pulling away.*]

GEORGIE: You don't want me, you know. You want Antonia. Now she's gone you've fallen in love with her all over again.

MARTIN: It's possible – yes. [*Without condescension.*] You're a clever girl. Sometimes I must have behaved as if you weren't. The circumstances didn't help. Too much sex for the time and space we've allotted ourselves.

GEORGIE [*softly*]: As if I didn't know that.

MARTIN: Oh, Georgie, Georgie, I want to do something for you, I want to *give* you something. What can I do? [*He thinks.*] I know. Take you to Hereford Square.

GEORGIE [*rather startled*]: Do you mean this afternoon?

MARTIN: Yes – *now*.

[*She sits up straight and puts her hands on his shoulders, considering him gravely.*]

GEORGIE: Surely that wouldn't be wise?

MARTIN: Don't worry. Antonia won't turn up. She's gone to a matinée.

GEORGIE: No, no. It's something else. Do you really want to see me there so soon? [*They look carefully at each other.*] Don't misunderstand me, Martin.

MARTIN: I don't misunderstand you. You mean it might upset me to see you there. Quite the contrary. It will be good, Georgie. It'll be – liberating – natural. It'll break down some of the – doubleness.

GEORGIE: You don't think you might feel resentment?

MARTIN: No, no. I'm sure I shan't. Besides, I want you to know that Hereford Square really exists.

GEORGIE [*softly*]: Yes. I do want to know that it exists. But not yet, Martin. I'm not ready yet to go through the looking-glass – into your other world. I'm too frightened. You could see me there as an intruder.

MARTIN: No.

GEORGIE: Yes. You easily might. And as for breaking down the doubleness, my dear, we can't really do that until we stop telling lies. Can we?

MARTIN [*rather impatiently*]: Well, it will symbolise breaking down the doubleness. I want to see you there, Georgie. It will do something very important for me to see you there.

[*He pulls her to her feet.*]

GEORGIE [*really alarmed*]: Martin, don't press me. I don't want to go. Not now. I feel superstitious about it.

MARTIN: You make me all the more determined to take you, you primitive child! I tell you, it will *help* me. I need air, Georgie. I need to recover a sense of freedom. Seeing you there will open up a new world.

ACT ONE

GEORGIE [*shaking her head*]: If you insist –

MARTIN [*going for his overcoat*]: I do. Let's go.

GEORGIE [*putting on a coat and her old scarf*]: I feel that if we go to Hereford Square something disastrous will happen.

MARTIN: Nonsense! [*Then he notices the scarf, with a flash of temper.*] Oh, not that old scarf! I buy you a beautiful new scarf –

GEORGIE [*with a flash of temper too*]: And I've worn it several times. But if I'm to go to your house, then this goes with me. It's part of the me that tried never to think about you in Hereford Square.

[*They go out together.*]

SCENE VII

The Lynch-Gobbon's drawing room, half an hour later. Everything is as before, only dustier and bleaker. There is no fire, and the room looks old and uninhabited. Outside a few snowflakes fall in the yellowish dusk. Throughout the scene there is an eerie pale winter light.

The room is empty for a few moments. Then MARTIN *and* GEORGIE *come in on tiptoe. Both are wearing overcoats, but* GEORGIE'S *scarf is loose, and before she begins moving around she puts it down in a prominent place. As soon as* GEORGIE *has taken in the room, they look at each other for a moment. Then she begins moving slowly about, touching things here and there as if to make sure they are real.* MARTIN *watches her, speaking slowly and quietly.*

MARTIN: Poor old house. It isn't itself any more. It's all damp and shivering, all unhinged and bewitched and strange. All desolate and dusty. This isn't ordinary

45

dust, though. It's not the kind you can brush away and make things bright again. It's another kind, like grey sleeping-powder raining down from nowhere, dulling everything, tarnishing everything. How is it that houses know? Houses know and rooms know when something in them has died. They sicken. They wilt and they mourn – becoming not the same any more – under a spell, under a sad, sad spell.

GEORGIE [*stopping, turning*]: Do you hate seeing me here?

MARTIN [*moving his arms as if liberated*]: No. I can't tell you how entirely good for me it is to see you here. But there's – so much pain too.

GEORGIE: I know. Don't be angry with me because of the pain.

MARTIN: Ah – I'm a long way from that. I feel more like kissing your feet. You've put up with so much from me, my dear. You've suffered and hidden your suffering.

GEORGIE: I didn't mind suffering for you. I almost want to say I enjoyed it. Yet that couldn't be true. And I doubt if anyone has the right to say it unless they're Jesus Christ. I think it only comes into my head to say it now because I half imagine the suffering is over. But that's stupid, isn't it?

MARTIN: Ah – [*He makes a rather hopeless gesture.*]

GEORGIE: I'm sorry. [*Then quietly, with a gesture at the room.*] I think you're hating me.

MARTIN [*as she begins wandering again*]: No.

GEORGIE: It's so strange and moving to be here. I can't think what it's like. It's like possessing you retrospectively. No, not quite that. But you've no idea how completely I assumed that I'd never see this place. I *will* now come to believe – and this will be so much better, oh so much better – I *will* believe that in the past, all that time you were away from me, you really went on existing. You existed *here*. It was just too painful to believe at the time. But I knew that it was wrong not to believe it. Not to believe it was a failure of love. Now, if you can help me, I can set that right. I shall love you better – much better, Martin – in the future.

MARTIN: Come over here. [*He leads her to the mantelpiece.*] I want you to *touch* all these things. [*He draws her hand towards an ornament, but she pulls it back.*] Yes, I want you to touch them. Then it will be complete.

GEORGIE [*muttering*]: Yes – but it could be sacrilege – I could suffer for it –

MARTIN: No. A good sacrilege. You bring me near to reality. You've always done that for me. Please.

[GEORGIE *hesitates. He takes her hand again and lays it on one of the ornaments. After a moment she moves quickly along the mantelpiece, touching all the objects. She looks at her hand.* MARTIN *takes it and kisses it in the palm.*]

MARTIN: There — I was right to bring you, wasn't I? [*She moves into his arms, but a sound beyond the door makes them spring apart.*]

MARTIN [*whispering, urgently*]: My God – that was someone unlocking the front door – it must be Antonia – [*He pulls her towards the French window.*] You'll have to go through the gate at the bottom of the garden. Then cut into the square and take a taxi home. I'll join you as soon as I can –

GEORGIE [*trying to escape his grip*]: No, no.

MARTIN [*pulling her to the window*]: Go at once, damn you!

GEORGIE: No, I don't want to. Let me stay and meet your wife. I won't be made to run away.

MARTIN: Do as I tell you!

GEORGIE: I haven't any money.

MARTIN: Here. Come on. [*He drags her roughly through into the garden.*]

[*The door opens and* HONOR KLEIN *stands there, looking in.* MARTIN *comes hurrying back, breathing hard, and is about to welcome Antonia when he sees who it is.*]

HONOR: Good afternoon, Mr. Lynch-Gibbon.

MARTIN [*recovering himself*]: Can I do anything for you, Dr. Klein?

HONOR: You mean – why the hell am I here.

MARTIN: Precisely.

HONOR [*holding up a key*]: You wife lent me a key to your front door. To recover a basket I'd lent her that she left here. It's of no particular value, but I use it all the time for books and notebooks. [*She has now come into the room.*]

MARTIN [*confused because he has noticed* GEORGIE'S *scarf still lying prominently in view*]: I see. Yes. A basket.

HONOR: It's there.

[*She indicates the basket, which has been unobtrusively visible throughout the scene. Hoping now to be rid of her he picks up the basket, but when he turns with it he sees that she is now close to the scarf. He hands over the basket. She nods her acknowledgment, then looks at the scarf, then at him.*]

MARTIN [*hurriedly*]: I'm rather proud of this house, actually. It belonged to my father, you know. It's a sort of family house, you might say. But of course you're not seeing it at its best. It's a bit shaggy now, and dusty, not quite itself. A fine morning in spring or autumn – a summer night when we're having a party – using the garden too –

[*His voice fades out as she continues to regard him gravely.*]

HONOR: A fine house I can see, Mr. Lynch-Gibbon. And full of beautiful things. Spring mornings, summer

evenings, it must be delightful. I was admiring the unusual archway in the hall – but of course this is not its moment. Perhaps it's a little – taken by surprise. And in need of cleaning. [*She runs a finger along the back of a chair in the direction of the scarf, then picks up the scarf and draws it through her hand.*] You mustn't let it – deteriorate. I hope this house is soundly built. For I think we're going to have a hard winter. A very hard winter. It's beginning to snow, Mr. Lynch-Gibbon. Perhaps you'll find you'll be needing this. [*She hands him the scarf.*] I'm sorry I – disturbed you. Good afternoon, Mr. Lynch-Gibbon.
[*She leaves him alone in the darkening room.*]

END OF ACT ONE

ACT II

SCENE I

Palmer's study the following morning.

PALMER *and* ANTONIA *are sitting together on the divan. They are upright, grave, noble. They hear something, look towards the door, look at each other, then towards the door again.*

MARTIN *enters, in a bustling sort of way, wearing an overcoat. They regard him gravely.*

MARTIN [*as he comes in*]: Well, my friends, here I am. But I warn you I can't stay long. Must look in at the office – last day of the year and all that sort of thing. [*He sits down on an upright chair in front of them. Then he realises something is wrong.*]
What's the matter? You sounded damned odd on the telephone. What's happened?

PALMER [*to Antonia*]: Shall we tell him?

ANTONIA [*intensely*]: Yes, of course.

PALMER: Martin – we have found out about Georgie Hands.

MARTIN [*aghast*]: Oh – for – [*but he controls himself.*] I see. You know about Georgie. [*He gets up.*]

PALMER: You're not going?

MARTIN: No, but you keep this room too hot. [*He takes off his overcoat and throws it down before returning to his chair.*] Who told you about her?
[PALMER *looks at* ANTONIA, *but she turns her back. He looks at Martin.*]

PALMER: That doesn't matter – just now.

MARTIN: Well, what have you found out?
[PALMER *looks again at* ANTONIA, *who replies, full of emotion, over her shoulder.*]

ANTONIA: Everything, Martin. Everything, everything, everything.

MARTIN: Well, there's no need to make such a fuss about it.

[*She makes a sound of distress.* PALMER *slightly shakes his head, then regards Martin gravely, tenderly.* MARTIN *makes an impatient movement to avoid this look.*]

MARTIN: I think I'd better go. [*He bolts for the door.*]

PALMER: Hold it, Martin. You can't go now.

[*He pauses to give Antonia a chance to speak, then continues as Martin swings round.*]

I'm afraid we can't just leave this thing.

MARTIN: I could –

PALMER: No, use your common sense, Martin – of course we can't. We have to talk about it, react in an honest way, bring it all out into the open.

MARTIN: And who's going to enjoy that – except you?

PALMER [*ignoring this*]: We can't pretend not to mind. Antonia has a right to hear from you on this.

MARTIN: To hell with Antonia's rights. Antonia's forfeited her rights.

ANTONIA [*still turned away, almost tearful now*]: Martin, don't be rude and unkind as well.

MARTIN: I'm sorry I said that. I'm suffering from shock.

PALMER: Antonia is suffering from shock too. You must be considerate, Martin. Now we don't want to be unpleasant and censorious. But we must have this thing right out. See?

MARTIN: I see. All right. Suppose you go away and let me talk to Antonia.

PALMER: I think she'd prefer me to be present. Isn't that correct, dear?

ANTONIA: Yes, of course.

[*She turns to face Martin now but does not look at him.* PALMER *puts an arm round her protectively.*]

MARTIN: What is there to talk about? You have the facts – and I don't deny them. Do we have to have the bloody court-martial as well?

PALMER: You misunderstand us, Martin. There is no question of a court-martial as you call it. Who are we to be your judges?

MARTIN: I don't know.

PALMER: We don't want to condemn you. We want to help you. But you must realise two things: first, that we both love you very much; and secondly, that you have deceived us on a matter of very great importance.

ANTONIA [*tearfully*]: Martin, I can't tell you how it hurts.

MARTIN: I'm sorry, my dear.

PALMER: Ah, but are you? And *do* sit down – it's so difficult – you know – having to look up –

[MARTIN *sits down.* PALMER *continues in his most solemn manner.*]

PALMER: We thought we knew you, Martin. We have just had a surprise. I won't say we're disillusioned – but I'll admit we're distressed. We have, in a sense, to start again. We've lost our grip. We have to see where you are. We have to see *what* you are.

MARTIN: I'll talk to Antonia but not to both of you.

PALMER: We are both wounded.

ANTONIA [*looking at him now*]: Martin, how *could* you have told such lies? I was so *surprised*. I know I sometimes tell lies myself, but I thought you were so truthful. And I thought you loved me so much. [*She sobs this.*]

MARTIN [*irritated*]: I did love you so much. I do love you so much. I just loved Georgie as well.

PALMER: And still do?

MARTIN: And still do.

ANTONIA [*bursting out*]: Honestly, I just can't think how you were capable of it.

MARTIN: My God – one can love two people. *You* ought to know that.

ANTONIA: All right, all right. But when Palmer and I told you about us, that you shouldn't have been honest *then*! I just can't conceive how you could sit there pretending to be virtuous – and let us carry all the guilt. It's not like you, Martin.

PALMER: No, indeed, it isn't like you. And yet it must belong to you.

MARTIN: No analysis, if you don't mind.

PALMER: Even analysts can get surprises. Well, it humbles one. We must just try again to understand you. For – *understand you we will.*

MARTIN [*confused*]: Look – I'm sorry. But I can't explain. Though there is an explanation. Or I think there is. It doesn't matter.

PALMER: But it does matter, Martin. It matters very much. Between us three every single little thing matters. And this is a very big thing. And we're in no hurry. If necessary we can talk about it all day.

MARTIN: Well, I can't.

ANTONIA: Martin, darling, don't pretend to be a cynic and not to care – it just doesn't ring true. We know you love this girl – why I can't imagine but I'm sure you do – and we do sincerely want to help you and the girl. Only you must be more frank and simple with us now.

PALMER: Antonia has been very honest with herself and with me. We have talked the whole thing out together. And you have no resentment to fear from either of us. We want in fact to – well – to give you our blessing. So you see how wrong you were and how unjust to us.

ANTONIA [*who has been nodding agreement*]: We'll stand by you and Georgie. We'll see you through, Martin. So please don't be guilty or worried, my dear heart.

MARTIN: I won't be guilty or worried, I'll be raving mad. I don't want you to see me through. I want you to leave me alone.

PALMER: You don't, you know. You only think you do. This unfortunate discovery has cast a shadow on us all – and we must all work together to remove that shadow.

MARTIN: You mean I must be tidied up so that you and Antonia can go ahead?

PALMER: You must be tidied up, as you put it, for your own sake as well. A lot of lying *must* be compensated for by a lot of truth-telling. I'm sure Georgie will agree with us. And then we shall be much happier, all four of us.

MARTIN [*explosively*]: You were on about all three of us a minute ago. Now it's all *four* of us. Why do you leave your sister out? Let's have a quintet.

PALMER [*even more stiffly*]: Come, be serious, Martin. You must take some responsibility for what you've done. As I said, we've got to understand you. And we shall understand you a good deal better after we've met Georgie.

MARTIN: Over my dead body.

PALMER: Antonia has only just heard of this young woman. It's very natural she should want to meet her. And you can both be thankful she will do so in no spirit of anger.

ANTONIA: I'm told she's beautiful and very clever – and

young, which is a lovely thing for you, Martin. Can't you see that I mean what I say? Can't you be generous enough to receive the gift of my goodwill – my blessing?

MARTIN [*going for his overcoat*]: I tell you I shall go raving mad.

PALMER [*who is smiling, his arm round Antonia*]: Now – now, Martin – you must understand –

MARTIN [*putting his overcoat on*]: Drop it – drop it! You talk as if you were arranging my marriage. [*Turning at the door.*] After all – for God's aske – you're not my parents. Or are you?

[*In the moment of pause before* MARTIN *goes out,* PALMER *and* ANTONIA *rise and draw together in a parental attitude, as if blessing him.*]

SCENE II

Georgie's room, the afternoon of the same day. The place is very untidy; books and papers are strewn about, together with used cups, empty glasses and overflowing ash trays. GEORGIE *herself looks tired and dishevelled. She is working at a table, but slowly, mechanically, without real interest.*

MARTIN *enters in a hurry.*

MARTIN [*urgently*]: Antonia knows. How did she find out?
   [GEORGIE *stares at him, unable to reply.*]
   And where were you last night, anyway, and then this morning? I looked for you everywhere and rang you up a hundred times.
   [GEORGIE *begins to get up slowly.*]
   Well, how did Antonia find out about us? Do you happen to know?

[*Standing now*, GEORGIE *rubs her face.* MARTIN *raises his voice and glares at her.*]

Come on, Georgie, snap out of it. Do you happen to know how Antonia found out?

GEORGIE [*slowly*]: I think so – yes.

MARTIN: Well?

GEORGIE: Honor Klein must have told her.

MARTIN: I don't see that. I'll admit that she saw your scarf – but what would that prove?

[*He takes it from his pocket and hands it to her.*]

GEORGIE: I told Honor Klein.

MARTIN: About us?

GEORGIE: Yes. Everything.

MARTIN: Good God! Why?

GEORGIE: Give me a cigarette, please. I don't seem to have any left.

MARTIN [*as he does and lights it for her*]: The Old Year's last surprise – *I hope*. What an extraordinary thing to do! Would you mind explaining?

GEORGIE: After you pushed me out of the house, I didn't go straight home. I felt too angry. I went and had a coffee, and then I came back. I felt bloody miserable and I rang you up but you weren't there.

MARTIN: I was out looking for you.

GEORGIE: Anyway, I'd just put the phone down when the doorbell rang. I thought it was you. Well, it was Honor Klein – looking as grim as hell. I asked her in and gave her a drink and we made some conversation. Then she suddenly asked me about you.

MARTIN: Just like that – bang!

GEORGIE: Yes. So I told her.

MARTIN: You mean – it all came out – the lot?

GEORGIE: Yes – the lot.

MARTIN: But – for God's sake, Georgie – *why*?

GEORGIE [*angrily*]: Because it was impossible to lie to her.
[*As he stares at her speechless, she does not look at him but
begins poking about the room.*]

I'm looking for a clean glass.

MARTIN [*angrily*]: If you're not insane, then you're start-
ing to behave like a treacherous little bitch. You let
that woman bully you.

GEORGIE [*with increasing emotion*]: I was tired of the
bloody lies. And I was so angry with you about what
had happened. It would have been so much better if
you'd let me stay. I simply loathed that whispering
and being shoved out at the back, as if you'd been
caught kissing the housemaid. I *hated* it, Martin! Do
you want a drink?

MARTIN: Not at the moment, thanks. All right, she saw
your scarf and guessed something. But why should
she trouble to follow it up?

GEORGIE: I don't know, *I don't know.*

MARTIN: You didn't ask her?

GEORGIE: Of course not! I said she carries too many
guns. I just told her – and it was a blessed relief!

MARTIN: A relief! You knew how important it was to
me that this shouldn't come out, especially now. I
simply can't cope with Antonia's knowing about it.
And you go and blurt it all out to this bloody woman
just because she was your supervisor at college. I don't
understand you.

GEORGIE [*violently*]: No, you certainly *don't* understand
me, and you've never tried to. I put up with things
being secret when they had to be, but I *loathed* it. I
suffered all the time, every bloody day! But I offered
you this suffering, gladly, because I loved you. Then,
when it didn't have to be secret any more and you
still kept on – it made me feel as if you were ashamed

57

of me. It began to poison things. Oh, I don't mean
you should instantly have married me, why the hell
should you? But there was no need to keep me so
deeply buried. And you *ought* to have told Antonia
then. I began to feel I didn't exist. I love you – yes,
I do love you – and I wish I didn't. I just feel utterly
poisoned. Oh – I would never have blown the gaff of
my own accord. But when Honor Klein came like
that, it was as if – oh – there was a message from the
gods. I *couldn't* have told lies then, I would have died
of it!

MARTIN: My God, darling, you don't know what you've
done. But it doesn't matter. It's my fault anyway. I
should never have put you in this position at all.

GEORGIE [*in tears*]: You're saying you don't love me and
you never loved me.

MARTIN: *I am not*, Georgie, you absolute sweet fool –
[*He puts his arms round her, but she stands stiffly.*] You
know perfectly well that I love you – but please be
rational now and *help* me. It's just that there's something *terrible* for me about those two knowing, about
the *way* they know. They were eating me up before.
Now they can assimilate me entirely. If I'm not care-
ful I'll go down like a dozen oysters.

GEORGIE [*a little calmer*]: What's so dreadful about the
way they know. You see, I do want to understand.

MARTIN: Oh – it's how it's all so hideously caught up
with their kind of intimacy and love. You'd have to
see it. It's like the nursery. For instance – and this is
God's truth – she's dying to meet you. Honestly –
dying to meet you!

GEORGIE [*jerking back, sharply*]: Is she? Well, that's
fine.

MARTIN [*hastily*]: Don't be silly, darling.

GEORGIE: I'm dying to meet her.

MARTIN: Don't *you* start.

GEORGIE: When you took me to Hereford Square you took me through the looking-glass. There's no going back. I've had enough of having things around that I'm afraid to think of. You can introduce me to her as soon as possible – *now* –

MARTIN: Not now, not ever. When you two meet, it'll be over my dead body.

GEORGIE: Don't be silly. [*She turns away resolutely as if about to get ready to go.*]

MARTIN [*impressively*]: Georgie, I am not going to introduce you to Antonia – and that's *that*.

[*As he stands commandingly and she fumbles for her coat, the scene blacks out. There is loud music that soon begins to falter and die.*]

SCENE III

Palmer's study, the same evening.

Under bright lights, ANTONIA, GEORGIE *and* MARTIN. ANTONIA *has dressed with care.* GEORGIE *is ostentatiously shaggy.*

MARTIN: Antonia, this is Georgie Hands. Georgie, my wife.

GEORGIE [*stiffly*]: Hello.

ANTONIA [*who is very nervous*]: How d'you do? [*She gives a little laugh.*] Well – that's that, isn't it? I'm so glad. I mean, I was so pleased when you rang up. You must have felt that, didn't you? Will you have a drink? Do sit down, please.

GEORGIE: No, thank you.

[ANTONIA, *anxious to please, moves rather nearer Georgie, then speaks in a tense little voice.*]

ANTONIA: Don't be angry with me.

[GEORGIE *shakes her head frowningly as if she found the remark absurd.* MARTIN *has been looking with some anxiety from one woman to the other.*]

MARTIN [*loud and clear*]: Well, Antonia, I'll have a drink. [*He helps himself; and continues to do so throughout the scene.*]

ANTONIA: May I call you Georgie?

GEORGIE: Yes, certainly. If you want to.

ANTONIA: And will you call me Antonia?

GEORGIE: Well – I don't know. Sorry – I don't think I can. But it's of no importance.

ANTONIA: It's of importance to me.

MARTIN: Oh – break it up.

ANTONIA: Martin, *please*! [*She puts a hand on Martin's arm, but looks at Georgie.*]

GEORGIE: Look – I wanted to see you, since you wanted to see me. I felt it was right – taking seriously what one had done.

ANTONIA: But of course.

GEORGIE: But I doubt if we can really *say* anything to each other.

ANTONIA: Don't dislike me, Georgie.

GEORGIE: Why should I? It's *you* who ought to be disliking *me*.

[MARTIN *removes his arm from Antonia's pressure.*]

ANTONIA [*warmly*]: Ah – you mustn't feel any guilt.

GEORGIE [*coldly*]: You misunderstand me. I was just replying to your remark. I wasn't implying anything else. I don't feel any guilt. I realise that I may have harmed you, and I admit my responsibility. But that's quite another matter.

ANTONIA: Don't be so harsh with me, my child.

GEORGIE: Sorry. I wish you well. Perhaps you wish me well. It's just that it's difficult to talk.

ANTONIA: Oh – surely it needn't be. I do wish you well – I *do*. I wish both of you so well. I hope you and Martin will be very very happy.

MARTIN: Leave me out of it, Antonia.

ANTONIA [*with a little laugh*]: What on earth can you mean – leave you out? How can you, between *us*, be left out, my dear? [*She takes his arm again, turning to Georgie with gay feminine appeal.*] Isn't he absurd?

GEORGIE: I don't think so.

ANTONIA: But how *can* we leave him out?

GEORGIE: He means there's nothing to discuss and some subjects are better not touched on. [*She gives Martin a look, and he frees his arm again.*]

ANTONIA: But Georgie, there's *everything* to discuss.

MARTIN [*with a falsely brisk air*]: Perhaps we'd better go now. You've set eyes on each other, which was what you were so keen about. Enough, enough! [*He finishes his drink and puts his glass down.*]

ANTONIA: Oh, don't go. I haven't had anything like enough of simply *looking* at Georgie. You must forgive me, child. You mustn't be embarrassed by the foolish way I go on, must she, Martin? I mean well, I really do. Please, *please*, sit down and drink some sherry. It's particularly good sherry, isn't it, Martin?

MARTIN: Yes – but a little too full and rich for this time of day –

GEORGIE [*cutting in, to him*]: I think I ought to go. Will you come with me or stay here? I really don't mind which you do. [*She turns to Antonia.*] It was kind of you to ask me. I'm glad to have met you. It makes things more honest.

ANTONIA: My dear child, I'm so glad too. You must learn to be patient with me. You *will* learn.

GEORGIE: I doubt if we shall meet again. I didn't enjoy deceiving you. And now I really must go.

[*She retreats,* ANTONIA *follows,* MARTIN *hovers behind Georgie.*]

ANTONIA: No, no – and don't speak of our not meeting again, why that would be too cruel. When you're married to Martin we shall often meet. I love Martin too, you know – I do. Really I think I love him better than ever.

GEORGIE [*firmly*]: That is nothing to do with me, Mrs. Lynch-Gibbon. And as for my being married to Martin, it seems to be very unlikely that this will ever happen. In any case it's no-one's business but our own. I hope I haven't been rude. If I have, I apologise. I must go. Thank you very much for asking me. [*She turns to go, with* MARTIN *hustling her and* ANTONIA *protesting. But before they reach the door it is flung open and* PALMER *makes a big entrance, all charm and high spirits.*]

PALMER [*gaily*]: Why – I nearly missed her. A patient delayed me. They're so demanding. [*He looks at Georgie admiringly.*] Forgive me for being so informal, Georgie Hands. I believe we have a lot of friends in common.

GEORGIE [*staring at him*]: Yes – I think so –

MARTIN [*gloomily*]: She knows your sister.

GEORGIE [*rather shy now*]: I saw you at a party once, in Cambridge. But you wouldn't remember me. [*She holds out a hand.*]

PALMER [*taking her hand, not shaking it*]: I do now – I do. Across a room, wasn't it? And now we can start getting acquainted. [*He is still holding Georgie's hand and staring at her with admiration.*] Well, Martin, I congratulate you – I most certainly do. You're a lucky man. Now I must insist on my rights. Georgie Hands, I forbid you to talk of going yet –

GEORGIE: Well – I don't know –

MARTIN [*fighting a losing battle*]: I do. I'm afraid we must be off.

PALMER: I don't believe it. We must all have a drink. Georgie Hands, sit down while I attend to you. Antonia, you too, darling.

[*He places* GEORGIE *in the chair, now exerting the maximum pressure of charm. The two women, after their scene together, seem glad to submit to it. But* MARTIN, *though he is no longer at the door, is still standing, away from the group.* PALMER *now serves the drinks as he keeps on talking quickly, not risking silence and changes of mind.*]

Haven't we all been forgetting – I know I have – what day it is? In six hours – nearer five hours – it'll be New Year's. Aren't we going somewhere tonight, Antonia darling? The theatre and some enormous party, isn't it?

[ANTONIA *begins to sob uncontrollably. As* MARTIN *hastens to her,* GEORGIE *rises abruptly, seizes her coat, and rushes out.* MARTIN *hesitates, and then runs after* GEORGIE. ANTONIA'S *sobs begin to grow into hysteria as* PALMER *moves smoothly towards her and the scene fades.*

Almost immediately the lights come up in GEORGIE'S *room.* GEORGIE *runs in, locks the door, and stands with her back to it. After a moment* MARTIN *follows her up the stairs outside the room and tries the door handle.*]

MARTIN: Georgie . . . Come on Georgie, let me in!

[GEORGIE *moves away from the door, tense and unhappy.*]

MARTIN [*banging on the door*]: Georgie! I know you're in there – Come on! Georgie! Georgie!

[*She does not answer, but remains rigid in the middle of the room.* MARTIN *waits for a moment, and then goes away down the stairs with a gesture of despair.*

The scene darkens. Sounds of New Year celebrations are heard. A church clock chimes the half hour.]

SCENE IV

Palmer's study, in darkness, just before midnight. There are continuing noises of New Year celebration.

MARTIN *is seen to enter against the light from outside. He blunders about cursing and talking to himself and looking for the electric switch. He eventually finds it and switches on a light, which brilliantly discovers* HONOR KLEIN *sitting at the other end of the room. A Japanese sword, in its scabbard, lies on the table in front of her. She sits without moving, a strange and impressive figure.*

MARTIN [*very startled*]: Oh! – Sorry, I didn't know you were in. [*Pause.*] Happy New Year. [*Another pause.*] I came back – wanted to see Antonia – to see Antonia and Palmer. [*He looks round, then – lamely.*] They don't seem to be about. Do you mind if I help myself to a drink. I think there's some brandy somewhere –

[HONOR *regards him without moving her head and says nothing. After a moment he begins rather awkwardly to look for the brandy.*]

MARTIN: Where are they anyway?

HONOR: At the opera.

MARTIN [*scandalised. He feels they ought to have been waiting for him*]: At the opera! What's on?

HONOR: *Götterdämmerung.*

[MARTIN *laughs, and is about to pour out a glass of brandy, but stops and looks at Honor.*]

MARTIN: Will you join me?

HONOR [*after a pause, as if giving him her attention with diffi-culty*]: Yes. Why not.

[*He pours out another glass. There is silence between them for a while. Each is self-absorbed.*]

MARTIN: You didn't waste much time in having me brought to justice, did you?

HONOR [*smiling faintly*]: Was it unpleasant?

MARTIN: I don't know. I suppose so. Everything's so unpleasant nowadays it's hard to tell.

[*They do not look at each other, and have an air of soliliquis-ing. The scene proceeds in a dream-like manner.*]

MARTIN [*after another pause*]: I'm a broken reed after all. Still no *violence* I'm afraid. Too bad.

HONOR: It will come, Mr. Lynch-Gibbon, it will come. We have a *rendez-vous* with it.

[*The bells sound louder in the distance.*]

[*As if to herself.*] It's almost the turn of the year.

[*They listen in silence.* MARTIN *becomes interested in the sword, which* HONOR *is holding in a predatory way with both hands on the scabbard.*]

MARTIN: Is the sword yours? [*He puts one hand on it.*]

HONOR [*she starts and draws it away*]: Yes, it's a Japanese Samurai sword, a very fine one. I have a great inter-est in Japan. I worked there for a time.

MARTIN: You were with Palmer in Japan?

HONOR: Yes.

MARTIN: May I see the sword?

[*For a moment she seems to ignore him. Then, suddenly, un-expectedly, with a frightening flash of energy she twists the scabbard on the table and rises, drawing the sword with a rapid flourish. She lets it descend more slowly and lie along her thigh. She contemplates it.*

HONOR [*drily, as if in the lecture hall*]: In Japan these

swords are practically religious objects. They are forged not only with great care but with great reverence. And the use of them is not merely an art but a spiritual exercise.

MARTIN [*he moves his chair so as to see her better. He sits at ease*]: So I've heard. I'm not attracted by the idea of decapitating people as a spiritual exercise.

HONOR: Being a Christian you connect spirit with love. These people connect it with control, with power.

MARTIN: What do you connect it with?

HONOR [*shrugging her shoulders*]: I am a Jew.

MARTIN: But you believe in the dark gods.

HONOR: I believe in people.

MARTIN: You sound like a fox saying it believes in geese. [*She muses, still self-absorbed. Then she suddenly whirls the sword in an arc that brings it close to the arm of Martin's chair. He obviously resists an impulse to move away.*]

MARTIN: I was a hero – that time. [*Rising and pushing the chair back.*] Now I'm going to flinch about a yard. Are you an expert Japanese swordswoman? You seem to be.

HONOR: I studied the use of it for several years in Japan. But I never got beyond the beginning.

MARTIN: Show me something.

HONOR [*coldly*]: I'm not a performer.

MARTIN [*drily*]: A pity. [*He finishes his brandy.*]

HONOR: Very well. I'll show you something. You see that figure of Bishamon – yes, that one. It's a bad fake anyhow – Palmer should never have bought it. Now – put your arm flat on the table and hold it steady. Yes, like that. But don't move. Keep it still. Don't tremble.

MARTIN: I'm not trembling. Get on with it.

HONOR: Keep still then.

66

[*She flashes the sword down and decapitates the figure, the head rolling to the ground. She remains a moment motionless as* MARTIN *rises slowly, taking his hand away from the headless figure.*]

MARTIN: Thank you. A wonderful trick.

HONOR: It was not a trick.

[*She sits down and cools her forehead on the blade of the sword. Then she lays the sword down upon the table, holding the hilt in one hand.* MARTIN *touches the blade, feeling the sharp edge almost up to the hilt.* HONOR *removes the sword and lays it across her knees.* MARTIN *rises.*]

MARTIN [*confused and still in a dream*]: I must go.

HONOR: You are not going to wait for your wife?

MARTIN: No. It's too late now. [*He looks at his watch.*] It's the New Year. Good night.

[*He slowly withdraws.* HONOR *is left, sitting like an idol with the sword across her knees. The bells grow louder. The lights fade out.*]

SCENE V

GEORGIE'S *lodging, the next day.* MARTIN *is seen climbing the stairs. He knocks, pauses and knocks again. He goes in and looks uncertainly about the empty room. Then, after a nervous glance at the door, he goes to the telephone.*

MARTIN: Hello, Antonia. Happy New Year. I rang this morning but you were out. . . . Yes, I'm at home. How are you? . . . Yes, I know. I terribly want to talk to you too, darling. How about this evening? . . . Not the opera *again*! . . . Well, how about after the opera? It wouldn't be too late? . . . Good. I tell you what I'll do, I'll bring round the wine I promised you. You remember, the Vierge de Clery '59. . . . No, no, darling, I insist on continuing your education. I think you'll find it an amusing wine. . . . Yes, darling, yes. Bless you. Tonight then. Goodbye.

[*He puts the phone down and ruffles his hair thoughtfully, a little ruefully. Then he finds a foolscap pad and begins to write a note to* GEORGIE. *There is a sound of laughter and chatter on the stairs.*]

GEORGIE [*off*]: It's not very grand, but I really do make excellent coffee!

[*Enter* GEORGIE *and* ALEXANDER. *General appalled amazement.*]

MARTIN [*to Alexander*]: What the hell are *you* doing here?

ALEXANDER: I just met Georgie at lunch today. Sorry, Martin.

GEORGIE: Why are you saying sorry? It's not very polite. There's nothing to apologise about. I brought Alexander back here for some coffee.

MARTIN: Why – have restaurants stopped serving coffee?

GEORGIE [*almost shouting*]: The coffee there was *bad* – and I said I could make much better coffee here –

ALEXANDER: Don't bother now, Georgie. After all, it's a shock to Martin – naturally.

GEORGIE: I can't see why. I've asked him about you often enough. He's only got himself to thank.

MARTIN: You two seem to be getting on splendidly together. May I ask how you ran into each other?

GEORGIE: Honor Klein introduced us.

MARTIN: That bloody woman again! I wish people would just stop interfering with my affairs.

GEORGIE: If people interfere with your affairs it's because you like it. You're dying to be interfered with. You're a sort of vacuum into which interference rushes. Anyway, it wasn't anything to do with you. Why do you assume everyone is so interested in *your* doings? You're not the centre of the world. Amazing as it may seem, people sometimes do things that have no connection with you whatsoever.

MARTIN: Yes, but not in the circle you've been moving in today – Klein and Company — Mischief Made to Order –

GEORGIE: I told her on the telephone I'd never met Alexander, so she very kindly invited us both to lunch with her. And I accepted. I'm a free agent after all. I'm not your slave.

MARTIN: If you're trying to hurt me, you're doing very well.

ALEXANDER: Go easy, Georgie.

MARTIN [*turning on him*]: I can do without kind words from you. You must know about Georgie and me –

ALEXANDER [*gently, apologetically*]: Yes. She told me.

MARTIN: Don't flatter yourself, she tells everybody. You seem to have had a jolly talk about me. And now will you please clear out?

GEORGIE: You're being beastly, Martin. It's not Alexander's fault. If you'd introduced us long ago instead of hiding me away this would never have happened. I didn't do it to hurt you. I just felt so damnably tied up, I had to do something to feel free.

ALEXANDER: And *that's* not very polite, is it?

MARTIN: You knew damned well I'd hate it. But perhaps we can continue this chat when my dear brother has gone.

ALEXANDER: Do stop being so intense, both of you. I don't know what's the matter with you these days, Martin. Where's your sense of humour? Do relax. Georgie, give him some coffee.

MARTIN: I'll thank you not to play the host in my own house.

GEORGIE [*shouting*]: It's not your house, that's the point!

MARTIN: Please go.

[ALEXANDER *bows, half ironical, half affectionately submissive. He looks at Georgie, smiling at her, admiring, rueful. She looks at him. It is clear they have had a good talk and like each other. Moving to go,* ALEXANDER *reaches out a hand and draws it slowly back over her head, feeling the shape.*]

ALEXANDER: Yes – yes. Perhaps this was the head I was waiting for.

MARTIN: Go – go – go.

ALEXANDER: Ah well. Georgie, thank you. Martin, sorry – oh – and a Happy New Year.

[ALEXANDER *goes.* GEORGIE *closes the door and moves into the room, watching* MARTIN *warily. He suddenly seizes her violently as if he were about to strike her; but instead he throws her on to the bed and strides angrily to the other side of the room.* GEORGIE *is close to tears, but controlled.*]

GEORGIE: I see the reign of terror has begun.

[MARTIN *now pulls her up to face him. She fumbles for a handkerchief.*]

All right, Martin – all right – all right – all right –

MARTIN: It's not all right.

GEORGIE: You don't understand. It was all much more accidental than it seems.

MARTIN: With that woman in it – never!

GEORGIE: Well, it was with me.

MARTIN: You oughtn't to have gone. [*He sits down, miserably.*] Oh well – it doesn't matter.

GEORGIE: It *does* matter. Martin, I'm miles nearer the edge than you've any notion of. I can't tell you how much I've suffered, not only from the lies but from

feeling so *paralysed*. I had to do something on my own.
I feel twice as real now. You've got to *see* me. You've
got to see what I'm really like at last. I suppose I'm
to blame. I've never been quite and entirely myself
with you. The situation didn't let me be. The un-
truthfulness infected everything. I had to break out
a little. Do you understand at all?

MARTIN: Yes – yes – yes. It doesn't matter.

GEORGIE: Don't keep saying that. And stop looking so
horribly dejected, for God's sake.

MARTIN: Anyway, the era of lies is over. We'll tell everybody now.

[*She is strangely silent. He looks at her.*]

MARTIN: You don't want it told now?

GEORGIE [*after a pause*]: I'm not sure.

MARTIN [*after taking this in*]: Will you marry me, Georgie?

GEORGIE [*very moved, but resolute*]: You don't mean it,
Martin. You're just a little crazy at the moment and
jealous. Ask me again later if you still want to.

MARTIN [*shaken*]: I love you, Georgie.

GEORGIE [*with a dry laugh*]: Ah – *that*.

MARTIN [*appalled*]: Oh – Christ!

[*He covers his face. She sits beside him and puts an arm
round him. But he refuses to be pitied, and jumps up, ready
to go.*]

I'm going.

GEORGIE: Martin. You said you used to pass your girls
on to Alexander. Are you sure it wasn't that he always
took them away from you?

MARTIN [*slowly*]: You learn fast, don't you? Yes, that's
how it was. That's how it was really. Goodbye,
Georgie.

[*He goes. An outer door slams.* GEORGIE *stares after him
for a moment and then falls to her knees on the floor.*]

A SEVERED HEAD

SCENE VI

Palmer Anderson's house late that night. The stage is divided into an upper and a lower level. Above is Palmer's bedroom, which is lit, below is his study, which is in darkness. Upon a huge golden double bed PALMER *and* ANTONIA, *in dressing gowns, are immobile, gazing at each other. Then with dignity they embrace.* MARTIN *enters the study from the hall, staggering under a large crate of wine, which he puts down in the middle of the floor.* ANTONIA *hears him and lifts her finger.*

ANTONIA: That will be Martin. [*She calls.*] Who is it?

MARTIN [*below*]: It's me. I've brought the wine.

ANTONIA: Come up and see us.

MARTIN: Have you gone to bed? I'm sorry to come so late.

PALMER: It's not late. Come on up, Martin. Look, bring three glasses and one of the bottles. We simply must have a look at you.

[MARTIN *takes a bottle from the crate and makes for the stairs.*]

ANTONIA [*guiding Martin*]: We're here.

[MARTIN *enters the bedroom with bottle and glasses. Throughout the scene* ANTONIA *and* PALMER *sit together on the bed, occasionally touching each other.*]

ANTONIA: How very sweet of you to bring the wine. Are you all right?

MARTIN [*who is clearly very affected by what he sees*]: I'm fine.

PALMER: Let's have some straightaway! I love a dormitory feast. I'm so glad you've come. I've been looking forward to you all day. Oh dear, there's no corkscrew! Do you mind fetching one?

MARTIN: I always carry one. [*He opens the bottle.*]

PALMER: I'm afraid we're offending against all your canons! Do you mind drinking it cold? Do pour out. [MARTIN *pours out the wine. He contemplates* PALMER *and* ANTONIA.]

MARTIN: Mars and Venus.

PALMER: But you are not Vulcan, are you, Martin? [MARTIN *gives them the wine.*]

MARTIN: I can hardly get higher than this.

PALMER: You are very high indeed, and we love you for it. We are all very high. This constitutes an apex.

MARTIN: That suggests a descent on the other side.

ANTONIA: Let us call it a plateau. People live on plateaus.

MARTIN: Only people with a good head for heights. Isn't it odd. Here I am bringing you wine in bed. Instead of which I ought to be wringing both your necks.

ANTONIA: Martin darling, you're drunk. Shall I order you a taxi to go home in?

MARTIN: Don't bother, I have the car. [*He moves to go, and knocks over the bottle of wine.*] Damnation, I've spilt the wine.

ANTONIA: Don't worry, my darling! It'll come out! [*She fetches a cloth and basin and mops up.*]

PALMER: And if it doesn't come out we'll put a rug over it. I forbid you to worry about it, Martin. But my dear fellow, can you get yourself home safely? Shall I drive you?

MARTIN: No, of course not. I'm perfectly capable. I'm terribly sorry about the carpet. I'd better go. I've left the crate of wine in the study. Will it be all right there?

PALMER: If you *wouldn't* mind just putting it in the cellar. Don't think of unpacking it, just shove it down there and leave it. It's very kind of you indeed.

MARTIN [*to Antonia, who is still mopping the carpet*]: I'm terribly sorry.

ANTONIA [*she kisses his cheek*]: You're not to worry. Is he, Palmer? Promise? Everything's all right.

MARTIN: I promise. I won't worry. Everything's all right. [ANTONIA *sees him to the door. There is a last golden tableau of* ANTONIA *and* PALMER *together. Then the bedroom is darkened. A moment later* MARTIN *re-enters the study and tackles the crate of wine. After a struggle involving collisions with furniture he stumbles, cursing, and dumps it on the floor. He examines a tear in his trousers. He stands a while in thought. He discovers the wine glass which he has absently put in his pocket. He opens another bottle of wine, pours himself a glass and broods over it. He starts at a sound from the back of the room. Enter* HONOR KLEIN.]

HONOR: Oh, it's you. I saw the light and thought it might be my brother.

MARTIN: Your brother is in bed with my wife. I just took them up some wine.

HONOR: You are heroic, Mr. Lynch-Gibbon. The Knight of Infinite Humiliation. One hardly knows whether to kiss your feet or recommend that you you have a good analysis.

MARTIN: You seem to dislike me nearly as much as I dislike you, Dr. Klein. But with less reason. I may be a fool but at least I don't meddle in your affairs. Not content with informing Palmer and my wife about Georgie and me, you then kindly introduced my brother to my mistress. Charming!

HONOR [*after a moment*]: She asked me to.

MARTIN: And you complied with alacrity! I wonder why? Why? Am I to credit you with a kind heart, perhaps?

HONOR: Don't waste the little irony you have. I did it

on the spur of the moment. I thought it was time for
her to see a new face. It doesn't matter.

MARTIN [*his anger growing*]: It matters to me! I wonder
if you have any idea what a destructive person you
are? *Damnably* destructive! I'd be obliged if you'd
keep your hands out of my affairs in the future.

HONOR: I have no wish to be concerned in your affairs.
I am going away. It is unlikely we shall meet again.

MARTIN: I hope you're right. And the further away the
better! I'm not the only one who'll heave a sigh of
relief, I can tell you.

HONOR: What do you mean?

MARTIN: Palmer – Antonia – all of us are sick to death
of you hovering over us night and day like a carrion
crow.

HONOR: You are drunk, Mr. Lynch-Gibbon. Foully
drunk. And even when you are sober you are stupid.
Please get out of my way.

[MARTIN, *who is barring her exit, doesn't move.*]

MARTIN: No, not drunk, Dr. Klein. I've been drinking,
certainly. A man escaping from women – must drink.
But actually I'm in a condition – we haven't a name
for it – when I'd be happier if I'd either had less or
had more.

HONOR: I think that describes you at all times, Mr.
Lynch-Gibbon. Goodnight.

[*She attempts to pass him.*]

MARTIN [*seizing her wrist*]: Wait a minute! Wait a minute!

[*She pulls her wrist free and slaps his face.*]

I'll let that pass – but don't try it again – *my darling* –

HONOR: Get out of my way – [*She tries to push past.*]

MARTIN [*as he stops her*]: Oh – no. Oh – no. There are
some more things I've got to say to you –

[*He grips her arm as she tries to reach the door. She shakes him off, but he seizes her again. A wrestling match begins. They struggle in silence, knee to knee, face to face, and then fall struggling to the floor. He captures her wrists at last and, kneeling above her, strikes her in the face. After a pause he rises and stares down at her, dazed. She rises more slowly and dusts her clothes.*]

HONOR [*she has somehow retained her dignity during and after the struggle. Without looking at him*]: Now – go away. At once.

MARTIN: Yes – of course. I'm sorry. Odd, isn't it? I came to that – rendezvous – after all. But I didn't think it would be like this. [*She does not speak, does not look.*] Goodnight.

[*She stands motionless, still not looking at him. He goes quietly and the light fades.*]

SCENE VII

The Lynch-Gibbons' drawing room on the next day. MARTIN *is reading a letter.*

ANTONIA [*voice only*]: Martin darling, it *was* lovely to see you last night. Please *don't* worry about the stain on the carpet – it's bound to come out, and even if it doesn't it will remind us of you. This is just a little note to say that if you want us don't ring Palmer's as we shall both be away for a few days. Mother isn't at all well so I'm going down to see her and Palmer has to be in Cambridge, so there'll only be Sister Honor holding the fort. Try to rest, darling – and don't be unhappy. We'll soon be back. Loving you, Antonia.

ACT TWO

[MARTIN *doesn't know what to do with the letter. On an impulse he crumples it up, then smooths it out again, then bundles it into his pocket and pours himself a large drink. He looks dishevelled and distracted.* ROSEMARY *enters bringing a cup of coffee.*]

ROSEMARY: I knew you'd like some coffee, Martin.

MARTIN: Thank you, flower. You're very kind. I mean it, very, very kind.

ROSEMARY: I wan't to help, dear. I feel we all ought to help each other.

MARTIN: Not all, no. Some of us ought to try leaving each other alone. I don't mean you, of course. How could I, when you come specially to this ruin to cook me a wonderful dinner?

ROSEMARY: But you didn't eat *anything*, Martin dear. You hardly touched the *paella*.

MARTIN: I know, I know, it's a shame – but I really wasn't hungry. I'm not feeling at all well, as a matter of fact. Are you *sure* my temperature was normal?

ROSEMARY: Below, dear. Now drink up your coffee and don't fuss. I want to leave everything tidy for Mrs. Thing in the morning.

MARTIN: Rosemary – flower – sister dear –

ROSEMARY: Yes, dear?

MARTIN [*carefully*]: Do you ever feel you are going out of your mind?

ROSEMARY [*briskly*]: No, I don't think so – never – why?

MARTIN: You never feel that things are getting out of control – that causes may no longer produce effects – that we may have come to the end of the reign of natural law, that from now on all is chance, random . . .?

ROSEMARY: Martin, you're in one of your silly moods. Have you been drinking again?

77

MARTIN: Yes, all day. But it hasn't done any good. I really think I must be going mad. I can't eat, I can't sleep, I can't read. And if I go to the cinema I feel like bursting into tears. What's the *matter* with me, flower?

ROSEMARY: Antonia ought to answer that –

MARTIN: It may sound odd, flower – but it's as if there were some sort of barrier across my path – something enormous – which I can't recognise yet. But somehow I feel that when I do, everything will make sense again.

ROSEMARY: I wish I could help you, dear – but I don't think I can. You'll have to work it out for yourself. I must fly now – don't bother about the washing-up, Mrs. Thing'll do it tomorrow. And don't worry too much, dear. Go to bed early, get a good night's sleep, and it'll all seem quite different in the morning. I always find it does! Goodnight, darling.

[*She gives him a quick kiss and goes out.* MARTIN *pauses for a moment, and then darts to pick up some letters he has written. The first runs into several pages.*]

MARTIN [*reading*]: Dear Dr. Klein, I literally do not know how to apologise for what happened last night. Perhaps all I can do is to offer some explanation of my extraordinary conduct –

[*He quickly flicks over the pages that follow, then tears them all up and picks up the next letter.*]

MARTIN [*reading*]: Dear Honor Klein, there is little point in trying to explain my conduct of last night. I cannot account for it; nor would you be interested in an implausible rigmarole about the state of my psyche. It is enough to have assaulted you, without boring you into the bargain. [*Pause.*] I offer you my humble and sincere apologies. I assure you that my contrition

78

burns. . . . [*He looks up again, stares ahead, then rapidly tears up the letter and picks up a third.*]

MARTIN [*reading, with increasing speed and agitation*]: Dear Honor, I am sorry that I behaved to you like a beast and a madman. I can offer no explanation, nor is this in the ordinary sense an apology. I feel that things between us, after last night, have passed beyond the region of apologies. [*Pause.*] I want to write you something brief and honest instead. [*Pause.*] In the past you have behaved with hostility towards me and deliberately done me harm. [*Pause.*] This does not, of course, excuse my having thrown you to the ground and beaten you about the head. [*Pause.*] I only write down here what seems to be the truth – and I am confident . . .

[*He crumples the letter and begins pacing the room, struggling with an emotion which he only half understands. He pours another drink but feels sick as soon as he tastes it. He goes to the window, throws it open and peers out into the mist as if striving to penetrate it. Then he moves to the desk, picks up his pen, and with a trembling hand begins to write a fourth letter.*]

MARTIN: My dear Honor. . . . My dear Honor. . . . My dear . . .

[*He slowly looks up, with the air of a man who has had a revelation, and his glance falls on the telephone.*]

MARTIN [*in a whisper*]: Honor, my dear . . .

[*He picks up the telephone and dials. His hands are trembling so much that he has to make three attempts before he gets the number. The telephone rings in the darkness in Palmer's study. After a moment, HONOR enters in a dressing gown, turns on the light and picks up the receiver.*]

MARTIN [*in extreme agitation*]: Hello . . . Honor? . . . Hello . . . Hello . . . Hello!

[*Without replying,* HONOR *puts down the receiver, leaving it off the hook, and begins to mount the stairs to the bedroom.* MARTIN *drops his own receiver to the floor, grabs his overcoat and rushes out. The lights fade in both rooms.*

In the darkness Palmer's telephone begins to emit the strange disembodied howling sound of the 'unobtainable' signal. There is a confused noise at Palmer's front door and MARTIN *is heard calling softly, 'Honor! Honor!'*

MARTIN *bursts into Palmer's study, and stumbles about in the dark trying to find the light switch. He strikes a match. There is a candle on the table, so he lights it. He replaces the telephone receiver on the hook. Silence. Carrying the candle he goes to the inner door at the back of the room, knocks, and looks inside – there is nobody there.*

Breathing heavily he begins to mount the stairs to Palmer's bedroom. The candlelight flickers eerily on the walls and his movements take on the quality of a dream. He reaches the landing and knocks on the bedroom door. There is no answer, so he flings it open and steps in. Revealed in the candlelight are HONOR *and* PALMER *embracing in bed.*

After a moment MARTIN *closes the door, appalled, and runs down the stairs into the study. He goes to lean on the mantelpiece, hiding his face.*

Enter PALMER *in a dressing gown. He switches on the light. Then he closes the door, leans against it and looks at* MARTIN.]

PALMER: How did you know I was here?

[MARTIN *looks up, surprised, then collects himself and stares back without answering.*]

Well, it doesn't matter. You've found out what you came for. Are you going to tell Antonia?

[MARTIN *says nothing.*]

Martin? [*He comes closer.*] My half-sister, remember. We had two different fathers, two very different fathers. And this, as it happens, was the end of a chapter. The end, Martin, I assure you, the very end, the last page.

Do you believe me?

Let's have no nonsense here. What has happened is going to have very serious consequences. I'm not sure that you fully realise what you've done.

Of course I can understand your being – quite appalled. It's one thing to imagine – though God knows what you imagined and why you imagined – it's quite another thing to see.

But your feelings don't matter. The person we must think of is Antonia.

For her, this would not be like discovering some ordinary unfaithfulness. We have to do with something which could shake the mind to its foundations. What is at stake here, Martin, is not just Antonia's happiness but perhaps Antonia's sanity.

Martin, this is desperately grave. If you are as wise and generous – and as good – as we thought you – you will keep silent. The alternative is sheer destruction. And don't imagine that *you* could survive it. Martin, if you tell Antonia we are all of us done for. [MARTIN *quietly leaves the room.*]

END OF ACT TWO

ACT III

SCENE I

The Lynch-Gibbons' drawing room, thirty-six hours later. The room is in semi-darkness.

MARTIN is asleep on the sofa, half-dressed, with a rug over him. He is heard groaning and tossing. He repeats Honor's name.

Suddenly the doorbell rings urgently. MARTIN *sits up in a confused way, looks at his watch and shakes it.*

MARTIN [*calling*]: Just a minute! [*Muttering to himself.*] What on earth is the time. . . . How long have I been asleep? . . .

[*The door bell rings again.*]

MARTIN [*jumping*]: Christ! [*He calls.*] Coming!

[*He switches on a bright light. The room looks bleak and ghastly. Then he goes to the door. Enter* ANTONIA. *She looks wild.*]

MARTIN [*confused and sleepy*]: Good Lord! Hello, Antonia, how are you? What time is it?

ANTONIA: Ten o'clock.

MARTIN: In the morning or at night?

ANTONIA [*staring*]: In the morning.

MARTIN: But why's it so dark?

ANTONIA: It's very foggy.

MARTIN: What day is it?

ANTONIA: Thursday.

MARTIN: God, I've slept for centuries.

ANTONIA: Martin, did anything odd happen when I was away?

MARTIN [*waking up*]: Odd? No, not that I know of. Why?

82

ACT THREE

ANTONIA: Well, something must have happened. Or else I'm going mad.

MARTIN: You're not the only one.

ANTONIA: Have you seen Palmer in the last day or two?

MARTIN: No.

ANTONIA: Well, something's happened to him.

MARTIN: What?

ANTONIA: I don't know. But I felt it at once last night when I came back. It was like walking into one of those stories where someone is possessed by the devil. He looks the same and yet he seems a different person. It's as if a different personality inhabited him.

MARTIN: Oh nonsense! For God's sake, sit down, Antonia, and stop looking as if you were going to scream.

ANTONIA [*her voice rising*]: But he *is* changed. And he's turned against me!

MARTIN: Turned against you? Antonia ... please stop being intense. I'm not feeling at all well myself. Just tell me quietly and calmly what the hell you mean. And for Christ's sake *sit down*.

ANTONIA [*speaking quickly*]: It isn't anything concrete, and yet it's overwhelming. Honestly, Martin, I'm frightened of him. He's so *cold* – he doesn't say anything to me, he just keeps watching me as if I'd committed some frightful crime. And that awful Honor Klein is giving me the creeps – she seems to be everywhere at once like a sort of black cloud, and she keeps looking at me too, and I'm just terrified! [*She sits down on the sofa with a whimper.*]

MARTIN [*obviously shaken*]: Pull yourself together, Antonia. You're imagining things.

ANTONIA [*tearful*]: No, really I'm not. I wonder if anyone has told him some story about me?

MARTIN: What story could anyone possibly tell?

ANTONIA: Oh – I don't know. Nothing *true*, of course. Something about me and some other man, for instance. You know how people love to invent things. Somebody must have done something to put him against me. You haven't done anything, have you, Martin? No, of course you haven't, my darling – I know – you're so sweet. [*Pause.*] Perhaps he's going mad. Martin, did you know his mother went mad?

MARTIN: No, I didn't. Are you sure?

ANTONIA: He told me when I went to him – at Christmas. When it was all so – [*She bursts into tears.*] Oh, Martin, I'm so miserable.

[*There is a sound outside the door. They both turn and look. The door opens and* PALMER *enters slowly. He does seem a different person – no smile, no charm.*]

PALMER: Antonia.

ANTONIA [*submissively, rising*]: Yes, Palmer.

PALMER: I've come to take you away.

ANTONIA: All right, Palmer.

MARTIN [*as he steps between them*]: No, it isn't all right. Now stay there, Antonia – don't move. [*He goes nearer to Palmer.*] How did you get in? Have you started walking through locked doors now?

PALMER: Just keep out of this, Martin. You've meddled enough with things you don't understand. [*He looks coldly and commandingly at Antonia, who stands petrified.*] Put on your coat, Antonia.

MARTIN: You meddled in things *you* didn't understand when you destroyed my happy and successful marriage.

PALMER: Happy husbands don't keep little girls as mistresses. [*To Antonia.*] Come along.

MARTIN: She isn't going with you. Can't you see she's terrified of you?

ACT THREE

PALMER [*coldly*]: Martin, you and Antonia will do as I tell you.

MARTIN: Not any more. Poor old Palmer. Now get out.

PALMER [*looking at Martin for a moment*]: You are a destroyer, aren't you. [*To Antonia.*] Antonia, use your reason. I want to talk to you – and not here.

MARTIN: *Get out.*

PALMER: Not without her.

[*He moves forward.* MARTIN *moves too, pulls him round, and hits him.* PALMER *goes down, holding a hand to his face.* ANTONIA *gives a little scream.* MARTIN *bends over* PALMER.]

MARTIN: Are you all right?

PALMER: Yes, I think so. No serious damage. It just hurts like hell.

MARTIN: That was the general idea. Let me see. [*Taking Palmer's hand away.*] Hm. I'm afraid you'll have a tremendous black eye. I haven't got anything to put on it, I don't think. We'd better get you home . . . here . . .

[*He offers him a hand.* PALMER, *curiously docile, rises to his feet.* MARTIN *vaguely dusts* PALMER'S *clothes with his hands, as they speak.*]

MARTIN: Would you like some whisky – or brandy?

PALMER: No, thanks. I'd like to go home. Lend me a handkerchief, will you? I can't see anything at the moment.

MARTIN: Did you come in your car?

PALMER: No, I'll need a taxi.

MARTIN: I'll make sure you get one.

PALMER: Come and see me soon.

MARTIN: Yes. Sorry. I don't know. *Taxi!*

[MARTIN *has been bundling* PALMER *off.*]

ANTONIA [*as* MARTIN *returns*]: Well – that appears to be that.

MARTIN [*going straight to the whisky*]: What appears to be what?

ANTONIA: You've got me back.

MARTIN [*absently*]: Have I? Good. [*He drinks.*]

ANTONIA: One might almost say – a spell suddenly broken.

[MARTIN *considers this, holding up his glass of whisky.*]

MARTIN: The hard way. Not good. [*He drinks.*]

ANTONIA [*exalted*]: Yes, you've got me back, Martin darling. Oh my dear – so familiar – so close – so wonderful! You – *us* – again. But we never really lost touch, did we, darling? We never really stopped loving each other for a moment. I think it was marvellous, the way we kept in touch, don't you?

[*By now she is sitting on his knee.* MARTIN *absently strokes her hair, drinking whisky at the same time.*]

MARTIN: Oh yes . . . marvellous. Heigh-ho. All's well that ends well.

ANTONIA: Isn't it extraordinary? It's just as if –

[*The telephone rings.* MARTIN *detaches himself and picks up the receiver.*]

MARTIN: Hello . . . Oh hello, Alexander!

ANTONIA [*pleased*]: Alexander! Good! Give him my love. Tell him to come round and see us –

MARTIN [*into the telephone*]: Sorry! That was Antonia sending her love and saying you must come and see us. Yes, she's here. I've a lot to tell you about that, but it'll keep. Where've you been all this time anyway? . . . You sound very mysterious. What is it? . . . Come on, out with it . . . *What?* Good God!

ANTONIA: What is it? What's happened?

MARTIN [*into the telephone*]: Well done at last, brother! Jolly good! Who is the lucky girl? Do I know her? . . . *What?*

86

ACT THREE

[*He covers the receiver with his hand, and puts the other hand to his head, aghast.*]

ANTONIA: What *is* it, Martin?

MARTIN [*into the telephone again, falsely hearty*]: Sorry – I missed that bit . . . I'll wish you luck *now*. I can't think why you imagined I'd be angry. . . . No, no, no – you're a cure for both of us. . . . I tell you I'm *delighted* –

ANTONIA: *Martin*!

MARTIN [*still to Alexander*]: Yes, of course. She'll know in a minute, she'll be delighted too. . . . Yes, if you like. Where are you, anyway? . . . Well, why not come round now? . . . Yes, at once. I'll open some champagne. I tell you, I'm very pleased with you both. . . . Admit you're a fast worker! Be seeing you. [*He puts the telephone down, looking dazed with misery. Still not understanding,* ANTONIA *looks at him in alarm.*]

ANTONIA: What's happened to Alexander?

MARTIN: My dear brother is getting married to Georgie Hands.

ANTONIA [*horrified, violently*]: *NO*!

MARTIN [*surprised at her violence*]: You ought to be pleased. It removes temptation from my path. I've asked them to come round now to drink champagne. They're at Gloucester Road station and they'll be here in a minute –

ANTONIA [*furiously*]: You've asked them round *now*? You perfect fool! Have you no consideration. I'm going out. [*She turns away and makes for the door.*]

MARTIN [*calling as she goes*]: My dear, I didn't know you'd mind. I should have asked you – I'll entertain them alone if you like. Antonia – do please stay – Antonia –

[ANTONIA *glares at him, and then goes out, banging the door.*

87

MARTIN *stands rigid for a moment. Then he falls on his knees on the floor, covering his face. He says 'Oh, Georgie'.*

He slowly picks himself up and goes out dejectedly to fetch the champagne and glasses.

The front door bell rings. Making an obvious effort to be brisk and hearty he goes to let them in. We hear voices off but no words. Then he re-enters.]

MARTIN [*falsely gay*]: Come along – come along – you disgraceful people –

[GEORGIE, *better dressed than she was earlier, and* ALEX-ANDER *come in silently, talking off their coats.* GEORGIE *avoids* MARTIN'S *eye. Clearly the strain is great for all three.*]

MARTIN [*babbling*]: The champagne's waiting – not iced – cool, though – nine times out of ten good champagne's spoilt by being over-iced. Well – now –

ALEXANDER: So you forgive us? I was afraid you'd blow me out of the water.

MARTIN [*an heroic effort*]: Lunatics! Nothing to forgive! Georgie, my dear!

[*He kisses her awkwardly on the cheek. She shivers. He shakes Alexander's hand enthusiastically.*]

Alexander – you're dam' lucky.

ALEXANDER: I know I am. Life can be very sudden. But the fastest things are often the surest things –

MARTIN: Come on, Georgie, speak up. It's only your old friend Martin. So my headlong brother carried you off?

GEORGIE [*subdued*]: Well – yes –

MARTIN: Then you're lucky too. Come and sit down and we'll all have champagne. And you can stop looking as if you've been caught plundering the till.

ALEXANDER: Shy characters we are. Actually we're glad we told you. Where's Antonia? Have you told her?

MARTIN: Yes, indeed. She's delighted too. Just powdering

her nose. Be down in a minute. I'll give her a shout.
[*He goes to the door and nearly collides with* ANTONIA *as she sweeps in, determined to be gay.*]

ANTONIA [*in a high voice, hardly under control*]: Darlings – what a lovely surprise!

ALEXANDER [*submissively*]: I hope we have your blessing.

ANTONIA: My most hearty blessing! Can blessings be hearty? My blessing, anyway. Let me kiss the child. [*She kisses* GEORGIE, *who remains stiff. A strange look passes between* ANTONIA *and* ALEXANDER. MARTIN *opens the champagne and begins pouring out. As the others are not speaking, he babbles again as he pours.*]

MARTIN: Judging so far by touch not taste – I'd say – this is just about – the right temperature – for a decent bottle of champagne – not the usual party swill of course – twenty-two bob a bottle, sale or return. Now then –
[*They are all holding their glasses.*]
Let me be the one to say – a happy ending to a strange tale. From Antonia and Martin to Georgie and Alexander – love and good wishes and congratulations!
[*They clink glasses rather awkwardly and drink. Then there is silence.*]

MARTIN [*desperately, to Georgie*]: I say, Georgie, you're looking terribly smart. Quite the up-to-date girl! Do I mean up-to-date?

ALEXANDER [*trying to help, murmuring*]: There was a young man of Pitlochry, kissed an up-to-date girl in a rockery –

MARTIN: Oh, steady! [*Wildly.*] And talking of Pitlochry, when *is* the wedding and where will you be off to for your honeymoon?

ALEXANDER [*looking at Georgie, hesitating*]: Actually – we're going to – New York.

MARTIN: New York!
GEORGIE: New York.
ANTONIA: New York!

> [*She leaves the room abruptly, slamming the door.* GEORGIE *bursts into tears and fumbles for her coat. As she goes out too,* ALEXANDER *follows her.* MARTIN *looks up to find the room suddenly empty.*]

SCENE II

The Lynch-Gibbons' drawing room, an evening some days later. MARTIN *enters dressed in city clothes. He hangs up his coat and bowler.*

Enter ANTONIA. *She looks tired and bored, her usual radiance dimmed.*

ANTONIA: Oh, there you are. You're very late.
MARTIN: Yes, I got held up, I'm afraid.
ANTONIA: You seem to live at the office nowadays. I don't think you've got home early once this week.
MARTIN: I'm sorry, my dear.
ANTONIA: Did you have a good day?
MARTIN: Quite good. There's still an awful lot of arrears of course, but I'm catching up.
ANTONIA: Did you taste the hock?
MARTIN: No, that's next week. [*He sits down next to her with his drink.*] Did you have a good day?
ANTONIA: You can imagine what sort of day I had. [*She glances at Martin's evening paper.*]
MARTIN: Did you remember to take your iron tonic?
ANTONIA: Yes, horrible stuff. Did you find the phenobarbitone, by the way?
MARTIN [*vaguely*]: Yes. Yes, I did. It's on the dressing

table. [*Pause.*] Would you like an aspirin with your
drink?

ANTONIA: May as well. [*He gives her one from his pocket.*]
[MARTIN *has absently picked up a book.*]
Must you start reading the moment you get in? I've
been alone all day, except for Rosemary coming in
this morning. which hardly counts as a treat.

MARTIN: Sorry. [*He puts the book away.*]

ANTONIA: And why are you always reading *The Golden
Bough*? You never used to be interested in mythology.
And all those ghastly Japanese legends? You haven't
even looked at that book I got you about naval war-
fare in the eighteenth century.

MARTIN: Sorry, dear. I'll read it next. [*He closes his
eyes.*]

ANTONIA: And don't go to sleep, either. [*She glances at the
paper again, then looks up.*] Was it *this* morning we
should have taken the vitamin things?

MARTIN: No – tomorrow –

ANTONIA: I don't believe you remember. I know I don't.
Ever since I've taken them alternate mornings I
doubt if I've taken any at all.

MARTIN: Tomorrow.
[*Pause.*]

ANTONIA: There's a parcel for you, by the way.

MARTIN: Oh – where?

ANTONIA: In the hall.
[MARTIN *gets up and fetches the parcel.*]

MARTIN: I've been thinking. Alexander was right.
Palmer isn't quite human.

ANTONIA [*keenly interested*]: When did Alexander say
that?

MARTIN: When he heard about you and Palmer.

ANTONIA: He was absolutely right – he very often is.

Palmer isn't quite human. And as for that half-sister
– straight from another planet, I'd say.

MARTIN: Yes.

[*They both sigh.*]

ANTONIA: They can both go to America or Japan or
Borneo and the sooner the better. I don't want to
hear of them, I don't want to know they exist.

MARTIN [*with a kind of sighing melancholy*]: That's what
will happen, my dear. You'll be surprised how soon
you'll forget.

ANTONIA [*irritably*]: Forget! Forget! We both seem to be
half-dead.

[*She looks at him impatiently while he picks at the string of
the parcel, lost in a melancholy reverie.*]

Oh – for God's sake – open your parcel.

MARTIN [*hastily*]: Yes – of course – [*He fumbles with the
string.*]

ANTONIA [*without any tenderness, anxiously*]: Martin – you
do love me, don't you?

MARTIN [*in a similar tone*]: Yes, yes, of course I do – of
course – naturally – of course.

[*They examine each other with curiosity and hostility. Then
they both concentrate on the parcel. He gets it open.*]

ANTONIA: What is it?

MARTIN [*uneasy, repelled*]: Can't imagine. Some sort of
queer stuff. . . .

[*He puts the box on a stool and pulls from it a long strand of
dark hair.* ANTONIA *comes to his side to look more closely.*]

ANTONIA: It's hair – human hair –

MARTIN [*staring at it, disgusted*]: Human hair? [*Then he
recognises it.*] My God – it's Georgie's hair!

[*He rushes for the door.*]

ACT THREE

PALMER'S *bedroom an afternoon three days later.* GEORGIE *is sitting up in bed, looking flushed, bewildered, frightened.* PALMER *is sitting beside her, leaning forward reassuringly.* HONOR *stands nearby, watching them in silence.*

PALMER: It's all right, Georgie, it's all right. It was just an accident, that's all.

GEORGIE [*she sounds like an over-excited child*]: Well, I felt such a sham when I came round. Really – in a way – it *was* an accident. Wasn't it, Palmer? I mean the first lot of pills I took wouldn't work so that I was still awake – but of course so muzzy I didn't really know what I was doing – and then–
    [*She is fingering her shorn hair.*]

PALMER: Quietly now, Georgie, quietly.

GEORGIE: And then I didn't know how many pills I was taking after that –

PALMER: Now, now. I'm the one who'll tell you when to talk. We'll have a lot of quiet now and a lot of talking later. We're going to be very honest and very lucid and bring everything out into the open and that's what will get us sorted right out.

GEORGIE: But I'm quite all right now – it was just an accident, that's all.

PALMER: Of course, Georgie, of course – it could have happened to anybody.

GEORGIE: But that's just what I mean. I mean, it's so good of you to have brought me here –
    [MARTIN *has entered the room, carrying books. There is a moment's pause as he looks across at Honor; then he gives his attention to Georgie.*]

93

MARTIN: Hello, Georgie. How are you?

GEORGIE: I'm quite all right, Martin. Palmer says it could have happened to anybody –

PALMER: Of course it could – anybody, anybody – but I must admit it doesn't always bring me in such delightful patients.

MARTIN: Georgie, I've brought you some books.

PALMER [*taking them*]: Books? Books? I don't think we need *books* just yet. Later on in the treatment perhaps, but not just now. No. No books. [*He hands them back to Martin.*]

GEORGIE: Of course it's absurd, this idea of my having to have treatment. I'm perfectly sane and in my right mind. I'm far saner than most psychoanalysts.

MARTIN: You could be too.

PALMER: Thank you, both of you! No doubt you are, Georgie. But it's just routine.

[*Enter* ROSEMARY *carrying flowers, followed by* ALEXANDER, *carrying chocolates.*]

ROSEMARY: Hello – may we come in?

[*A chorus of greetings from the group around the bed.*]

ROSEMARY: I'm not going to stay a *minute*, Georgie, but I did just want to say how sorry I am and that you mustn't worry because it could have happened to anybody.

ALEXANDER: Of course it could. To anybody.

PALMER: There, Georgie, it's the general opinion. And that's not always wrong.

HONOR [*murmurs*]: Not when it agrees with what we want to believe. . . .

[*Enter* ANTONIA *carrying a large toy wrapped in tissue paper. She looks gay and handsome.*]

ANTONIA [*pushing through the throng*]: My poor child! Darling, I can only stay a second. I've got an appoint-

ment at the hairdresser's. Now let me look at you.
Yes, it suits you. You were absolutely right to do it.
Doesn't she look ridiculously young? I've brought
you a little present, darling. I do hope you'll like it.
[*She has been unwrapping the parcel, revealing a large pink
and white rabbit.*]

PALMER [*taking it from her*]: Perfect – just perfect. Here
Georgie; something to pet, something to cuddle.

GEORGIE [*taking it*]: Oh, he's sweet! What shall I call
him?

MARTIN: Why not Sigmund Freud?

PALMER: Now listen everybody. It's wonderful to see
you and don't think we're not grateful, but Georgie
is my responsibility now, and we have to be very
firm, we medical men – we have to be tyrants.

ROSEMARY: Yes ... well, I must fly then. Goodbye,
Georgie. You and Alexander must come and have
tea, when you're up and about again. Martin, are
you coming?

MARTIN: No, not for a moment.

ROSEMARY: Goodbye, everybody. [*Chorus of farewells.*]

ANTONIA [*gaily*]: Well, my child, I can't sit staring at
you all day. I must dart off, darling.

ALEXANDER: I'll drive you. I have to see a man about
a head. You're looking wonderful now, Georgie.

ANTONIA: Yes, isn't she? Like one of those naughty little
French film moppets. Come along.

ALEXANDER: Goodbye, Georgie.

ANTONIA: Well, let's go.

[*She sweeps gaily out, followed by* ALEXANDER.]

PALMER [*to Martin and Honor*]: Now you kids run along.
I want to have a serious talk with my charming little
patient.

MARTIN [*who has been submissively departing, suddenly*]: So do I.

[*A pause. Then* PALMER *makes as if to interrupt, but* HONOR *imposes silence for* MARTIN.]

[*Softly, to Georgie*]: Listen, Georgie – before I lose sight of you altogether in this labyrinth, before you become altogether the other person that you've half become. You remember before Christmas when we sat in front of your fire, like two children in a wood? We must have had, mustn't we, such a lot of innocence then, as we've lost so much since. Perhaps we went too far into the wood, too far, like Hansel and Gretel, until we came to the witch's house. I'm not appealing to you, Georgie, and I'm not saying I'm sorry and I'm not saying goodbye. But I see you receding from me now into a world which isn't my world. It isn't your world either. I just want to say this: please at least believe in the past, don't let anyone ever persuade you that the past was false. For if they persuade you of that you'll break into little pieces entirely. That's all I want to say to you, and that's all I shall ever have of you now. Remember, Georgie. If you want to know why you did what you did, ask your own heart and don't take any other answer.

[MARTIN *marches quickly out of the room.* HONOR *stares thoughtfully after him, then follows him down the stairs.* GEORGIE *and* PALMER *draw together. The bedroom darkens.*

The lights change to the study below. MARTIN *enters from the stairs and goes to the far side of the room. When* HONOR *enters she closes the door behind her and leans against it.* MARTIN *turns, and they face each other across the room. Pause. Extreme tension.*]

MARTIN [*after a moment or two*]: I suppose you know that I'm in love with you.

HONOR [*as if after taking thought*]: Yes.

MARTIN: I doubt if you realise how much.

HONOR [*quietly but without weariness*]: It doesn't matter.

MARTIN: That I love you, or how much?

HONOR: The latter. I'm touched that you love me. That's all.

MARTIN: It's not all. I want you. I propose to fight for you. I shall fight savagely.

HONOR [*unimpressed*]: There's no place for such a love.

MARTIN: You have no right to say that. It would profit me little now if I were to tear your clothes off. But I would walk through fire if you called me.

HONOR [*attentive but cool*]: You don't know what you're asking. Do you want my love?

MARTIN [*startled*]: I don't know. I don't even know if I think you capable of love. I want you.

[HONOR *looks at him in silence. Then she laughs, throws off her coat, and pours out two glasses of sherry. She puts one glass on a table half way down the room and returns to her place.*]

HONOR: Martin, you are a perfect ass!

[MARTIN *fetches the drink and returns to his place. He is delighted by her use of his Christian name and by the fact that her hand trembles as she pours out the sherry.*]

MARTIN: Because I doubt your capacity to love, or because I want you?

HONOR: You don't know me.

MARTIN [*trembling. He puts the glass on the floor*]: Let me know you. I have an apprehension of you which is deeper than ordinary knowledge. I believe you realise this.

HONOR: It is no more than a dream. It does not inhabit the real world. Return to reality. Go back to your wife. I have nothing for you.

MARTIN: My marriage is dead. I love you and I desire you and my whole being is prostrate before you. *This is* reality!

HONOR: Not every love has a course to run, smooth or otherwise, and this love has no course at all. Because of what I am and because of what you saw – that night – I have become a terrible object of fascination for you. I am a severed head such as primitive tribes and old alchemists used, when they put a piece of gold on the tongue to make the head utter prophecies. And perhaps long acquaintance with such an object might lead one to a very strange knowledge indeed. For knowledge like that one would have paid enough. But that has nothing to do with ordinary love and ordinary life. As real people you and I just don't exist for each other.

MARTIN [*who has attended to her closely*]: With you I have at least paid all the time. You were right – I have paid as I earned. This precisely *does* make you real for me. You give me hope.

HONOR: I don't intend to. Be clear about that.

MARTIN [*flagging for a moment, and showing weakness*]: What can a love do which has no course to run?

HONOR: It becomes changed into something else, something heavy or sharp which you carry within you and bind around and around with your substance – until it ceases to hurt. But that is your affair.

[*After his sign of weakness she seems to regard the interview as at an end. She takes her glass from the mantelpiece and sips it. She fumbles for cigarettes. Then as* MARTIN *begins to advance towards her down the room she becomes rigid. He comes fairly close and they stare at each other. Then, without touching her he falls full length at her feet.*]

HONOR [*after a moment*]: Get up.

MARTIN [*now on his knees*]: Honor, please don't let us fight like this. Only see me a little. I only ask for that. I don't know your situation, I don't know what you want. But I feel so sure that this thing – this thing that has been shivering and trembling between us in these last minutes is a real thing. Don't kill it. That's all I ask.

[*He is abject now and she exasperated. The precarious spell is broken.*]

HONOR: We are not *fighting*. Don't deceive yourself. You're living on dreams. Get up. You must go now. Palmer will be down soon, and you have nothing to say to him. Go on.

MARTIN [*rising*]: But you'll see me again?

HONOR: I see no point in our meeting. Palmer and I are going away almost at once.

MARTIN [*imploring, not commanding*]: Don't speak to me like that – as if – as if –

HONOR: As if *what*?

MARTIN: I know. I'm being abject. I want you – even abjectly –

HONOR [*mockingly*]: Dear me, dear me, and whatever would you do with me if you had me?

[*He looks hard at her for a moment until the amusement dies out of her face, then bracing himself, he walks straight towards the door. Before he reaches it, PALMER opens it and comes in a step or so. MARTIN brushes him on one side without looking at him and goes out. HONOR stands and stares after him for a moment: then when PALMER appraoches, as if to discourage talk, she sits and picks up a book. As PALMER is thus checked and looks bewildered and irresolute, the scene fades.*]

SCENE IV

The Lynch-Gibbons' drawing room, early evening, two days later. MARTIN *is at the telephone.*

MARTIN: Hello. Well, for heaven's sake let me speak to the station sergeant. My name's Lynch-Gibbon. I've spoken to you before. . . . No, no, not a child. My wife – Mrs. Lynch-Gibbon. . . . Yes. You're sure there's no report – nothing from a hospital? I see. . . . Naturally I'm anxious – it's nearly two days now. . . . Well, you may be used to this sort of thing – but I'm not. . . . Very well. Thank you very much.

[*He puts down the receiver and paces about the room. Then* ANTONIA *bursts in, wildly elated.*]

ANTONIA: Martin – darling!

MARTIN: What the devil do you mean by this? I've been nearly off my head. Two days – no message – no telephone – nothing. Where the deuce have you been?

ANTONIA: We had to go *somewhere* to talk it all out, so we went to Midhurst – you remember that place – and now we're going to Rome – *tonight* –

MARTIN: What are you babbling about? *Who* went to Midhurst? *who's* going to Rome?

ANTONIA: Darling, we're going to have a drink now, a nice big one – and I'll tell you all about it. Sit down. Now what would you like, darling – sherry? Something with gin?

MARTIN: Yes, if you like. [*He looks at her ironically.*] Yes, you're looking your best. All right, all right, I'm glad to see you – and now will you kindly explain?

[*She pours out the drinks and comes to sit beside him. She gazes at him intently, sips her drink, and then pours the rest into his glass.*]

ANTONIA [*solemn now*]: Darling, I don't know how to say this, because I don't know how much you know.

MARTIN: Know about what?

ANTONIA: About me and Alexander.

MARTIN: You and *Alexander*? Are you sure you've got the name right?

ANTONIA: Yes of course. But surely you knew. You must have known for ages.

MARTIN: Known *what*?

ANTONIA: Well, that I and Alexander – well, to put it quite bluntly, that Alexander's been my lover.

MARTIN [*getting up*]: Oh – Christ!

ANTONIA [*quickly*]: You mean you didn't know at all? Surely you must have guessed.

MARTIN: Of course I didn't know. Do you imagine I'd have tolerated it?

ANTONIA: Well, you were so understanding about Palmer, I felt you must have known, you must have *understood*, about Alexander. Besides it was so obvious. And what do you mean by saying you wouldn't have tolerated it? I loved you both, you loved us both, Alexander –

MARTIN: Oh, don't start all that again. How long has this been going on?

ANTONIA: Well – really from the beginning. Alexander fell in love with me almost the moment we met.

MARTIN: So our marriage never really existed at all?

ANTONIA: Of course it did, darling. . . . Well, I suppose it could never have been *quite* right –

MARTIN: No marriage is ever quite right. But I believed in ours once. Now you tell me it wasn't there – what about Alexander and Georgie?

ANTONIA: Oh, that was sheer despair. Alexander was so hurt by the Palmer business. He started the thing with Georgie as a sort of distraction. And he was sorry for her when she fell so much in love with him. Then Georgie made that show of trying to kill herself, when she found out that Alexander really loved me. You see, I never really lost touch with Alexander, never –

MARTIN [*confused, horrified*]: Georgie now – next on the list – *bang*! – gone! –

ANTONIA: Poor Georgie. But she's young. She'll find somebody her own age

MARTIN: You must be pleased with yourself, Antonia. It turns out everybody loves you in the end.

ANTONIA: I *am* good at it. And don't resist my love, Martin. I must keep you in my loving net.

MARTIN: And we keep you in the family.

ANTONIA: You dear ironical creature! You move me so much when you try to conceal your goodness in that flippant way. You have a far, far better character than your brother, darling. Oh – I *do* love you – both of you!

[*She hugs him, lifting one foot behind her in an ecstatic girlish manner. He suffers her embrace.*]

MARTIN [*breaking into wild laughter*]: Well, aren't you a lucky girl?

ANTONIA [*not catching this, gaily*]: Aren't I a lucky girl!

[*She begins to embrace him again, but now ROSEMARY enters, carrying a small parcel and a letter.*]

ROSEMARY: Oh – hello! The door was open so I walked straight in. Martin, I've brought you two avocado pears.

[MARTIN *collapses, laughing hysterically.*]

They aren't *quite* ripe, but the man at Harrods said

they should be all right to eat in a day or two if you keep them in a nice warm room.

MARTIN: Thank you, sister. But you'd better give them to my dear wife. She's just off to Rome with our dear brother.

ROSEMARY: Oh – I don't know. It can be bitterly cold in Rome at this time of year, and Italian hotels are never properly heated.

ANTONIA [*still gay*]: Oh, Rosemary dear, you're marvellous.

MARTIN: Yes isn't she. It only remains for *me* to fall madly in love with *her* and then we can all go and live happily ever after.

ROSEMARY: Martin!

ANTONIA Well, darlings, I must grab some things and fly –

[*She darts off in a hurry.* MARTIN *and* ROSEMARY *look at each other.*]

MARTIN: You didn't happen to know about Antonia and Alexander, did you?

ROSEMARY: Well, I knew there was *something*. But I didn't know exactly what, and I didn't want to know, because I couldn't help feeling it might be disgusting. You must remember, Martin dear, I've never really liked Antonia – never. Oh – I found this letter on the mat. It must have been delivered by hand. [*She gives it to him.*]

MARTIN: Thank you, Rosemary of England dear, for your brave true thoughts. [*He sits down and opens the letter.*]

ROSEMARY: Don't be silly, Martin – not at a time like this. I was hoping Antonia would go off with Dr. Anderson. He wouldn't have cared how badly she behaved, being an American. And anyhow you and Alexander would have been rid of her –

[*But* MARTIN *is reading.*]

PALMER [*voice only – as Martin looks through the letter*]: Martin, we are flying to America tonight, and on from there to Japan. There is no reason why our paths should ever cross again; and you will understand me when I say that it will be better for us all if they do not cross. On what has passed you will not receive a commentary, from me or from any other. Let the dignity of silence cover like the sea an enterprise which, to an extent that I think even you never realised, partook of madness. Do not reply to this letter which constitutes, from both of us, a final and authoritative farewell. Palmer.

[MARTIN *pockets the letter and remains staring in front of him.*]

ROSEMARY [*gently*]: What is it, Martin dear? Tell me. A trouble shared is a trouble halved – even yet.

MARTIN: Palmer's going to America.

ROSEMARY: You don't care about *him*, do you?

MARTIN: No. Not about him.

[*No more can be said because now* ANTONIA, *dressed for travel, hurries in. Her mood is intense and tender now.*]

ANTONIA: I really must go now, Martin dear. I promised I'd pick Alexander up at his studio – [*She comes to Martin.*] Darling, you do understand – you *will* understand? I know this is mad – but it's the only thing to do.

MARTIN: Maybe. You're the expert. You'll need a taxi.

ANTONIA: I've had one waiting.

MARTIN: How confident you must have felt, Antonia dear.

ROSEMARY: If there's nothing I can do for you, Martin –

MARTIN: There isn't –

ROSEMARY: Then I'd like to see Alexander before he goes –

ANTONIA [*going*]: Come along then – [*To Martin.*] Martin, darling Martin, all right?

MARTIN: Oh, go to Rome, Antonia, go to – Yes, yes. Send me a postcard!

ROSEMARY [*as she goes*]: But don't expect it to be *warm* – it may be bitterly cold –

[*They go out, followed by* MARTIN. *and are heard departing. For a moment or two, the stage is empty. It looks desolate. This is clearly what* MARTIN *feels when he returns. Then the telephone rings.*]

MARTIN: Hello, London Airport? ... Oh, no, no, no, I'm afraid Mrs. Lynch-Gibbon's gone. This is her – husband speaking. Well, it must have slipped her mind. ... Yes, I can confirm her booking – two seats, to Rome, tonight. No, not me – my brother. Not at all, it was a pleasure. [*He makes to put the telephone down, but then hurriedly picks it up again.*] Hello! While you're on the line, I wonder – would you be kind enough to confirm that some friends of mine are on your night flight to New York? It's Dr. Palmer Anderson – and – his party. ... Oh, they're travelling ... gone aboard already. ... Also a Miss Georgina Hands, travelling with them to New York? No, no, I was only a little surprised. ... No delay? I'm very glad. ... A fine – clear night? ... Splendid. Splendid. Thank you.

[*He slowly puts down the receiver and moves around aimlessly, disconsolately. He pulls back the curtains to reveal the night sky. He stands looking up.*]

MARTIN [*murmurs*]: Goodbye ...

[*He sits down, utterly wretched. After a moment or two*

HONOR, *wearing an outdoor coat but no hat, enters quietly.*
MARTIN *looks up and stares at her, astounded, then slowly
rises.*]

MARTIN: I thought you were gone.

HONOR: As you see –

MARTIN: I've just spoken to London Airport – but I
didn't mention your name and they must have mis-
understood. Have Palmer – and Georgie – gone? [*He
indicates window.*]

HONOR: Yes.

MARTIN: How did you get in here?

HONOR: You must have been lavish with latchkeys. I
never returned the one Antonia lent me.

[*He has been in a daze so far, but now he comes out of it.
His manner is harder and more suspicious. He frowns at her.*]

MARTIN: When are *you* going?

HONOR: I'm not going.

MARTIN [*after pause, frowningly*]: Well, what are you
doing here?

HONOR [*after a slight pause*]: I came to see you.

MARTIN: Why? I'm the man – you remember, the abject
type – you dismissed the other day. So – why?

[HONOR *says nothing. Very slightly smiling, she sits down
and looks at him.*]

MARTIN: You're not going at all?

HONOR: Not at all.

MARTIN: How long is Palmer going for?

HONOR: For good.

MARTIN: So – it's finished – with Palmer?

[HONOR *says nothing. She continues to look.*]

MARTIN [*trying to work it out*]: And you yourself – what
about you?

[*She does not reply. She relaxes and crosses her legs.*]

MARTIN [*sharper now*]: Well, may I ask again why you're

here? If you've come merely to amuse yourself, to torment me, then you'd better clear out – now.

HONOR [*grave, but with a certain ironical lightness*]: I haven't come *to* torment you.

MARTIN: Oh – I realise it may happen inadvertently. I know you have the temperament of an assassin.
[*In spite of himself his expression lightens a little. They gaze at each other, still tense and serious.*]
But why, Honor, why? Why here? Why me?

HONOR [*she considers this; then*]: Have you ever read Herodotus?

MARTIN: Yes, a long time ago.

HONOR: Do you remember the story of Gyges and Candaules?

MARTIN [*recollecting*]: Yes, I think so. Candaules was a king and he had a beautiful wife. He was so proud of her that he wanted his friend Gyges to see her naked. So one night he hid him in the bedroom and Gyges saw. But the Queen found out about it and told Gyges that, because of what he had seen, he must either die or kill Candaules and become her husband and King himself.
[HONOR *is silent.*]
I see. Or do I? [*Pause.*] You once accused me of talking nonsense. If I'm only privileged because of – of what I saw –
[*He looks questioningly at her, but she is still silent.*]
You told me you were a severed head. Can one have human relations with a severed head?
[*She is still silent.*]
As you yourself pointed out, I hardly know you.
[*She is silent. But she is beginning to smile and so is he.*]
We have lived together in a dream up to now. When we awake will we find each other still?

[*She does not reply.*]

We must hold hands tightly and hope that we can hold on through the dream and out into the waking world.

[*She says nothing.*]

Could we be happy?

HONOR: This has nothing to do with happiness, nothing whatever.

MARTIN [*taking this in*]: I wonder if I shall survive?

HONOR [*smiling*]: You'll have to take your chance, won't you?

MARTIN: And so will you . . .

[*They approach each other at last as*
THE CURTAIN *begins to fall.*]